# WHY

## A Family Book of Knowledge

Octopus Books

# ABOUT THIS BOOK

Life consists of asking questions. We start from the moment we learn
to string words together and most of us go on asking them
for the rest of our lives. Alas, we don't always find the answers.

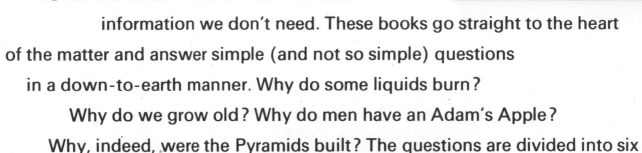

This book (and its companion volumes in this
series) presents a random array of questions
most commonly asked—and not only by children.
When a question springs to mind, ferreting
out the answer can be a difficult business.
Often the answer lies buried in a mass of
information we don't need. These books go straight to the heart
of the matter and answer simple (and not so simple) questions
in a down-to-earth manner. Why do some liquids burn?
Why do we grow old? Why do men have an Adam's Apple?
Why, indeed, were the Pyramids built? The questions are divided into six

Planned and created by
Berkeley Publishers Ltd.
20 Wellington Street, London WC2

First published 1974 by
Octopus Books Limited
59 Grosvenor Street, London W1
under licence from Lynx Press Ltd.
601 Union House
Hong Kong

ISBN 0 7064 0375 4

Printed in Czechoslovakia

main categories. There is no attempt to be definitive, for millions of
questions could be posed. With the help of a team of teachers and students,
we've picked out the ones most commonly asked—
and some that simply appeal to us. If you know the origin of
Easter eggs and can instantly explain why India has monsoons
then go to the top of the question class. If you can't, then welcome aboard.
Our family book of questions will be your
perfect guide and companion. If you can't find the
answer to your own particular question in WHY,
well then, try WHERE or WHEN or WHAT
And when you've exhausted *our* questions,
try dreaming up some of your own—
and find out
the answers for yourself!

# IN THIS BOOK

## Natural History

## People and Events

# Geography and the Earth

# The Body and Medicine

# Science and Technology

# General Knowledge

# Natural History

## FLOWER SCENT

The sweet scent of flowers is designed to attract insects who seek food in the shape of pollen and the fragrant-smelling nectar. This nectar is a solution of sugars produced in little sacs called nectaries at the base of the flower petal.

The insects have a part in the process of fertilization. Almost all plants perpetuate themselves by means of sexual reproduction, during which a male reproductive cell or sperm fuses with the female reproductive cell or egg.

When bees or other insects visit flowers in search of the sweet-smelling nectar, parts of their hairy bodies become dusted with pollen which contains the male reproductive cells. This rubs off on the flower's carpels which contain the egg or ovule.

Insects seem to be strongly attracted by sweet scents. In fact, some flowers, such as the Meadow Sweet, are so highly scented that insects are attracted to them although they have no nectar to offer. Most insect-pollinated flowers have evolved wonderful devices for guiding the movements of the insect. In this way they ensure that pollen is dusted over the insect's body.

## DINOSAURS

No one really knows the exact reason for the extinction of these gigantic reptiles. But many theories have been put forward to account for the dinosaurs' disappearance at the end of what scientists call the Cretaceous Age. This was about 70 million years ago.

Great catastrophes such as floods, earthquakes and volcanic eruptions producing deadly gas and ashfalls have been suggested. But such catastrophes would have had to be almost world wide since dinosaurs were present on all continents.

Food might have been a problem, vegetation underwent great changes during that period of the earth's history. Parasites and diseases might have struck the creatures down. Perhaps the dinosaurs, which were up to 80 feet in length and bulky in proportion, were unable to adapt themselves to the changing conditions.

The most plausible explanation may be that there was a great cooling of the climate. This would have affected the big dinosaurs much more than birds and mammals who could regulate their body temperatures.

A definite solution of the mystery of the death of the dinosaurs still seems far distant. It may have been due to a combination of some of the theories given here or of others still unknown.

Nevertheless the dinosaurs survived for more than 100 million years. We have been here for only two million years.

## DOGS IN MOULT

Dogs normally moult every year in late spring. As the weather becomes warmer the dog's body temperature is naturally kept down by the process of shedding hair. Dogs in moult should be brushed regularly, so that the old hair does not interfere with new growth.

dinosaurs die out? **WHY** do dogs moult?

Coelophysis

Tyrannosaurus

Diplodocus

Stegosaurus

# WHY does the spider family bear the name Arachnida? WHY
## WHY do penguins only have

## ARACHNIDA

Ages ago, people believed there was magic in the weaving of a spider's web and the Greeks told a story about a girl, Arachne, who was to give all spiders the name of Arachnida.

One day, Arachne, who was skilled in the art of weaving, challenged the goddess to a contest. She proved herself better than Athene at the craft and that immortal goddess, jealous and enraged that a mere mortal should defeat her, changed Arachne into a spider, eternally doomed to weave her web with the thread spun from her own body.

It is interesting to see how scientists have classified animals in order to bring out their natural evolutionary relationship. There are other creatures in the class of Arachnida, including scorpions, mites and king-crabs. Arachnida is grouped under Arthropoda, the class of animals with an outer skeleton made of chitin—a horny substance, the body divided into segments with jointed limbs. Arthropoda in turn comes under Metozoa—animals with bodies made up of many cells. Metozoa is one of the two main groupings of animals, the other is Protozoa which consists of very small, usually microscopic, animals found in fresh water or in the sea and having only one cell.

## SEPALS

The sepals of a flower protect it while it is in bud. The flower is really a kind of shoot, in which the leaves have been altered so that they can take on the task of producing seeds.

In a simple flower these leaves are arranged in circles, called whorls. The outermost are five green, leaf-shaped sepals. Inside these are five petals, usually heart-shaped, each with a small flap at its base where nectar is produced to attract bees and other insects.

Both the sepals and the petals are attached at their bases to the "receptacle", the swollen end of the flower-stalk, which looks like a cone in the middle of the flower.

Above the sepals and petals are the parts of the flower used in reproduction. These are the stamens, which contain the yellow pollen, and the carpels, which contain the ovules.

Most flowers are built on this plan but there are wide variations in size, shape and colour, and in the numbers of the different parts of the flowers.

## PENGUINS

Nearly all birds use their wings for flight, but penguins use theirs as paddles for swimming. They spend most of their lives in the sea and find their food there.

Although many birds can both swim and fly, no other bird can swim as well as the flightless penguins.

Penguins have muscles, bones and organs very much like those of flying birds, so we assume that their ancestors must have been able to fly. Probably they slowly lost the power of flight while learning to swim faster and dive deeper in search of food. This must have happened millions of years ago, for by Miocene times— 25,000,000 years ago—there were penguins very much like those alive today.

The feathers of penguins are short and grow all over their bodies, leaving no bare spots unprotected

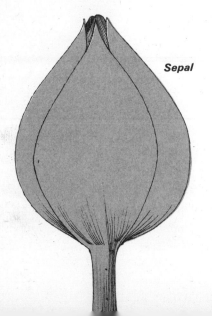

*Sepal*

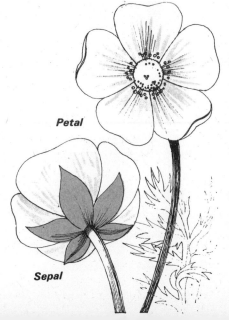

*Petal*

*Sepal*

do flowers have sepals?

small flipper-like wings? WHY do we have a dawn chorus?

## DAWN CHORUS

The song of the birds at dawn has given pleasure to millions of people and has been celebrated in poetry and prose for many years. The most usual explanation given in the Middle Ages was that the birds sang each day in praise of God and the beauty with which He had clothed the world. More recently, there was the feeling that the birds sang joyously to welcome the rising of the sun, which meant food, warmth and activity.

However, scientists now think that the dawn chorus is made up of the warning signals of each bird as he re-establishes his territory. The establishment of a territory for courtship, nesting and food getting is the first step in the breeding cycle and the area is defended against competing birds of the same species by a warning song, although seldom by actual fighting. A robin, incidentally, has a particularly strong sense of territory.

from cold air and water. The feathers of the paddle-like wing are small and stiff, with broad flat shafts. On the rear edge of the wing are rows of many short feathers with strong shafts.

The bones of the wing are flattened. This allows the whole wing to be thin and streamlined, but yet strong enough to push the bird through the water. Its shape is much like that of the flipper of a seal. Some of the bones have grown together, so that the penguin paddle is stiffer, though thinner, than the wing of a flying bird.

The breast muscles, which work the wings, are as large and powerful as those of any bird, but the muscles in the wings are small. Many of them are largely made up of slender bands of strong tendon. This, too, helps in making the paddle wing flat and thin.

# WHY are there "closed" seasons for game birds and certain WHY do flamingoes stand on one leg?

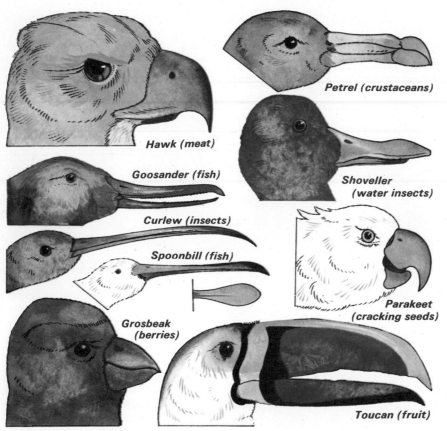

Hawk (meat)

Goosander (fish)

Curlew (insects)

Spoonbill (fish)

Grosbeak (berries)

Petrel (crustaceans)

Shoveller (water insects)

Parakeet (cracking seeds)

Toucan (fruit)

## BIRDS AND BILLS

The shape of a bird's bill or beak is closely related to the kind of food it eats and the way in which it collects or catches this food.

A crow or jay has a strong all-purpose bill, capable of killing small mammals but fine enough at the tip to pick up small insects. Many songbirds have slender bills for picking up insects from leaves or out of cracks; others have wide flat ones for catching flies or strong thick ones for cracking seeds and nuts.

Birds which dig for worms usually have long bills with sensitive tips while many water birds have broad dredging bills. Divers and grebes have straight spear-like bills and the birds of prey have strong hooked bills for tearing flesh.

Birds which catch insects on the wing (nightjars, swallows etc.) have tiny beaks but an enormous 'gape' by comparison.

## CLOSED SEASON

"Closed" seasons originated to ensure that a plentiful supply of game birds and animals could be guaranteed for the sportsman. The "closed" season is that part of the year when these animals and birds are protected by law and may not be shot or hunted for sport. If indiscriminate hunting was allowed during the breeding season, the survival of the species could be in danger.

The most famous game bird is perhaps the British red grouse. The date when the "open" season for shooting it begins is August 12, or the "Glorious Twelfth". The season closes on December 9. Another game bird, the partridge, is more unfortunate in Britain. Its "open" season lasts from September 1 to February 1. "Closed" seasons apply to many other wild creatures in a number of countries. Some animals are protected by law throughout the year.

## FLAMINGOS

Flamingos stand on one leg to relax the other.

"I must just take the weight off my feet" is an expression often used by people to explain why they must sit down. But even when we are seated our ankles may still support the weight of our legs, so we cross our legs to take this weight off the ankle.

We are not alone among animals in this wish to rest the ankles. A horse sometimes stands with only the tip of one hoof touching the ground and its weight supported by the other legs.

Flamingos and storks and other long-legged birds are more noticeable when they are standing in this relaxed position, for what appears to be their knee joint, half-way up the long legs, is in fact their ankle. Other birds relax in the same way, but with shorter legs the action is not so obvious.

animals? **WHY** do birds have differently shaped bills? **WHY** does wood rot?

## WOOD ROT

Wood rots or decays because it is an organic substance—that is to say, it is a living thing—made up of tiny box-like units called cells. Like any living things these cells can die. The attacks of insects and the growth of fungi are two of the most common causes of decay.

In leaves or flowers the cells are often square or rounded in outline. But in timber or wood they are mostly long and narrow, for they have to serve as tubes to carry sap from the roots up the tree trunk. Their walls are strong and fibrous because they have to support the weight of the branches and leaves above them. They interlock to form the wonderfully strong and pliable substance which we know as wood.

The cells do not continue to carry sap for the whole lifetime of the tree, because the trunk and boughs grow larger and soon contain more cells than are needed. So the inner part of the trunk and branches ceases to carry sap, and the cells gradually fill up with gums and resins which make them stronger, harder and better able to resist decay and rot.

When wood is cut the cells are full of watery sap. This timber is stacked in the open air for several months, or in a special drying-room, called a kiln, for several days. It is then "seasoned" and ready for use.

14

# WHY do many birds have honeycombed bones? WHY are
## WHY do plants flower at differen

## HONEYCOMBED BONES

Birds fly so well because they have developed skeletons which are especially light and strong. Most of their bones are hollow, with the interior webbed or honeycombed across by fine girders of bone to give added strength. They are sometimes called "pneumatic" or air-filled bones.

A bird's skull is made of thin bone in remarkable contrast to the solid, heavy skull of the mammal. The bones of its spine are flexibly connected in the neck, strongly bound together in the front part of the body and united at the rear into a solid, rigid mass. Powerful muscles attached to the breast-bone move the wings.

The bones in the wings have been reduced in number to provide greater strength. Wings can be used also as propellers. They can be shortened or lengthened by flexing, the feathers at the tips can be spread or closed, and the angle of the wings or their parts can be altered. All these adjustments make the aerodynamics of a bird's wings much more complicated than those of an aircraft. Consequently, the flight of a bird is more varied and adaptable.

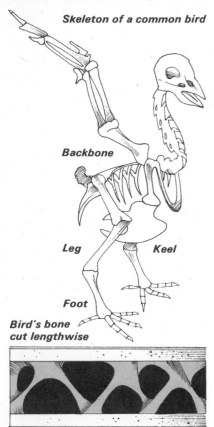

*Skeleton of a common bird*

Backbone

Leg          Keel

Foot

Bird's bone
cut lengthwise

## JAPANESE TREES

Many Japanese trees are small because they are dwarfed by the Japanese art of bonsai. This art consists in training and growing dwarf trees as symbols of the Japanese ideal of the immersion of the self in nature. This ideal also finds expression in their poetry, the tea ceremony and flower arranging.

The tiny trees express quietness, beauty of shape and line, and the changes brought about by the seasons. They must look old, with a sturdy yet shapely trunk which has bark of an interesting colour and texture, and well-exposed roots. There must also be a proper feeling of scale. This means short needles on conifers, tiny leaves on deciduous trees, and small flowers or fruit. Lastly, there must be open space between branches and between masses of foliage.

The word "bonsai" means tray-

nany Japanese trees small?

imes of the year? WHY don't trees grow on mountain tops?

## PLANTS IN FLOWER

The flowers appear at the times most suited to the production of seed for the continuation of the species. Before seed can develop the flower must be pollinated. This means that the dust-like pollen produced by the stamen of the flower must be transferred to the stigma of the ovary.

Pollination is brought about by various means. Most plants are pollinated by insects and, therefore, flower at a time when the insects are active. The flowers may have evolved a particular colour and scent to attract particular varieties of insects.

Five classes of insects visit flowers—Hamiptera (bugs), Coleoptera (beetles), Dipters (flies), Hymenoptera (bees) and Lepidoptera (moths and butterflies). Pollination by birds is widespread throughout the tropics and some animals, such as bats, also play a part.

Wind-pollinated plants include all the conifers, grasses, sedges and rushes, and many forest trees which tend to flower either early or late in the season when the chance of wind is greater.

If pollination by some other agent has failed, self-pollination will often take place at the end of a flower's life. This is usually brought about by movements of the stamens.

planted. The art goes back more than 1,000 years. It originated in China and spread to Japan in the 12th Century. During the 19th Century many Westerners came to admire bonsai. But it was not until the end of the Second World War that it became really popular in the western world. Bonsai societies were established in many countries, and many Japanese families now maintain a flourishing overseas trade.

## TREES ON MOUNTAINS

Trees do not grow on mountain tops either because the situation is too exposed, or because the soil is too thin or too frozen to allow their roots to draw nourishment from the ground.

In most mountainous areas there is usually a clearly marked timberline, a boundary above which there is no tree growth. Sometimes the height of the timberline is dictated by local climatic or soil conditions, but as a general rule the boundary gets lower as the distance from the Equator increases. In the far north and south the cold is so intense that it is quite impossible for any trees to grow, and the timberline is therefore at sea level.

A range of mountains on or near the Equator, like the Ruwenzori range in Africa, can be divided into different belts of vegetation according to the types of trees growing at its base and at various heights up its slopes.

Similarly the belts of vegetation change according to the distance from the Equator. The first belt is the tropical or rain-forest region where it is hot and trees grow rapidly. Next comes a hot dry belt where few trees grow because there is so little rain. This is followed by the deciduous or warm and temperate belt, and by the coniferous belt, with very cold winters but fairly warm summers. Then comes the timberline, beyond which trees cannot grow, and finally the regions of permanent ice and snow, where no vegetation at all can live.

# WHY do some plants capture insects? WHY do African

## INSECTIVOROUS PLANTS

Some plants capture insects and other tiny animals and use them as food. They do not devour their prey by chewing but decompose them in a mixture of enzymes. The pitcher plant attracts an insect to its large showy leaf by means of sweet-smelling nectar. The leaf has a treacherous lip which precipitates the unwary victim into a deep hollow pitcher full of a digestive 'broth', which soon decomposes its body. Other plants, like the Venus's flytrap, snap their leaves shut on their prey as it prowls about the trigger hairs glistening with drops of nectar. The sundews secrete a sticky fluid.

## ELEPHANTS

African elephants have larger ears than Indian, or Asiatic, elephants because they live in hotter conditions and are bigger and more aggressive and active. The huge ears of the African elephant, sometimes three and a half feet wide, enable it to hear more acutely. When the animal charges it fans out its ears, augmenting its terrible appearance and striking fear into the heart of any enemy.

The ears also present a large surface for losing body-heat. African elephants, who are at a disadvantage in the heat because of their large size, wave their ears to keep cool and to chase away flies.

The African elephant is the biggest and noblest of land animals, reaching a height of 11 feet and a weight of nearly six tons.

The Asiatic elephant is smaller. It inhabits the forests of south-east Asia from India to Ceylon and Borneo. It does not like heat and seeks the deep shade of the forest. The Asiatic elephant likes bathing, and showers itself with water sprayed over its back from its flexible trunk. For hundreds of years this elephant has been domesticated and used as a beast of burden, and its relationship with man can be close. Elephants are said to have excellent memories.

elephants have bigger ears than Indian elephants?

# WHY are crabs, lobsters and shrimps called crustaceans?

## CRUSTACEANS

The word "crustacean" comes from the Latin *crusta* meaning a hard covering shell or crust. Apart from crabs, lobsters and shrimps, there are thousands of different crustaceans. They live in the sea, except for a few species such as the common woodlouse.

Crustaceans differ greatly in size and shape. Many of them pass through remarkable changes of form (metamorphoses) before reaching the adult stage. All of them, however, have bodies and limbs which are divided into segments. All, too, are covered with a tough, hard, lime-impregnated coat, or shell, which is pliable at the joints, so that the creature can move its limbs.

This coat, or cuticle, cannot grow to fit its wearer. As its owner grows, it is split and cast off. A new coat, still soft and pliable, has been forming underneath, and may take several days before it hardens into a truly protective shell. During this time the creature is defenceless and may fall an easy prey to any enemy.

Vast numbers of crustaceans live in the oceans. They provide food for many kinds of fish and also for the largest living mammals, the whales.

## VAMPIRE BATS

Vampire bats are dangerous because they carry rabies and other diseases and infect their victims as they suck the blood which is their only food.

Vampire bats (Desmodontidae) are found only in South and Central America. They have extremely sharp teeth and pierce the skin of their prey so gently that the victim does not awaken. Blood is drawn into the mouth by the almost tubular tongue and the vampire bat's whole digestive system is specially adapted for his diet of blood.

# WHY are vampire bats dangerous?
# WHY do birds preen themselves?

## PREENING

Birds preen themselves to clean and waterproof their feathers, to maintain their general health and to keep them lying smooth and neat. This preening or grooming starts as the nestling's feathers are breaking out of their sheaths. The young bird spends a great deal of time combing the feathers with its bill and freeing them from bits of sheath and other blemishes.

In adult life the bird continues this behaviour and also uses the preen glands or oil glands which are located on the back, just in front of the tail. The birds nibble at the glands and rub their heads against them, spreading the secretion on their feathers. This oil waterproofs the plumage, keeps it supple and maintains its insulating qualities. The oil may also be useful as a source of Vitamin D if swallowed accidentally by the bird.

Many kinds of birds have preen glands. They often combine preening with dust or water bathing. Ducks may be seen dipping their heads under water, flicking their wings and wriggling their bodies while preening. This seems to give them great pleasure and fun.

## WOOD GRAIN

The grain in a piece of wood is the pattern produced by the annual bands or rings which grow in the trunk of the tree during its lifetime.

The tree's rate of growth varies with the seasons. In the spring soft porous wood is needed to carry sap. In the summer, stronger cells of hard wood develop to support the growing weight of new leaves and branches. The number of these alternate bands of soft and hard wood gives the age of the tree.

In close-grained wood, which has grown slowly, the annual rings are narrow and packed closely together. If the coarse-grained wood has grown more quickly, the rings are broader and spaced more widely apart. Sometimes the rings are irregular, and the grain may be straight, spiral, interlocked or wavy.

Skilful sawing is necessary to make the most of the grain and enhance the beauty of furniture made from the wood.

## YEW IN CHURCHYARD

Yews have long been associated with religious worship. So it is likely that churches were originally built near the sacred trees rather than the other way round.

These trees live longer than any other species in Europe and can grow to an enormous size. Many are thought to be well over 1,000 years old. Yews were revered by the druids of ancient Britain, France and Ireland and no doubt early Christian missionaries preached in the shelter of the trees before their first churches were built. Hywel Dda—Howell the Good—a Welsh king who reigned in the 10th Century, set a special value on "consecrated yews".

Some yews are even older than the ancient churches beside them, suggesting that the church was built on a spot already devoted to worship. The association continued, and it became traditional for yews to be planted in churchyards.

Also the great age to which yews live caused them to be regarded as a symbol of immortality and, therefore, associated with death, as man only becomes immortal after he dies.

Another theory is that yews were planted in churchyards so that they might provide wood for the longbows of medieval archers.

many old churchyards? **WHY** can owls see well at night?

## OWLS

The night vision of owls is 100 times as keen as that of human beings, because their eyes are especially adapted for seeing in the dark. But most are almost colour-blind and the pictures they receive are slightly blurred. This is because their eyes contain more rod-shaped receptor cells than cone-shaped ones.

Operating in bright light, cone cells sharpen details and react to colour. Rod cells gather light and owls have 10 times as many of these as do human beings. Each cell contains "visual purple", a substance capable of transforming the slightest glimmer of light into a sight impression.

Owls have exceptionally large eyes and can control the amount of light entering by expanding or contracting the pupil. Each pupil can act independently of the other so that owls can see objects in the shadows and in bright light at the same time. Owls' eyes are so large that they are supported by thin, bony, tubular structures called sclerotic rings. Because of this the eyes are almost immovable and nature has compensated for this by giving owls extremely flexible necks, which enable them to turn their heads through an arc of 270 degrees.

These birds have excellent binocular vision as their eyes are in the front of their heads. This gives them a tremendous advantage in swooping on small lively prey, because distance judgment depends on binocular vision. To add to their advantages at night, the owls have outstanding hearing, keener than that of any other carnivorous bird.

But owls can also see well in the daytime. Although most species hunt by night, others are active at dusk or in full daylight.

22

# WHY do some animals hibernate?    WHY are frogs, toads

## AMPHIBIA

The word amphibia comes from two Greek words: *amphi* meaning "of both kinds" and *bios* meaning "life". Amphibia are a class of vertebrate (back-boned) animals that can live both in water and on land. They are descended from fishes that lived more than 300 million years ago.

The first amphibia to crawl out of the water were heavily built, and slow and clumsy on land, but more active in water. They had long bodies and tails, and some developed into the highly efficient class of reptiles.

About 160 million years ago many amphibia became extinct. But a few survived to develop into the present-day frogs, toads, newts, salamanders and the worm-like caecilians.

Modern amphibia usually have moist, tough skins. They breathe partly through their skins, although they also have lungs. They usually lay their eggs in water. Here the young live, breathing chiefly through gills, until they change into their adult forms.

They eat insects, snails, worms and similar food, and are eaten by fish, snakes and birds. They are usually small. But the Giant Salamander of the Far East is $5\frac{1}{2}$ feet long and the Giant Frog of west Africa grows to a mature length of almost one foot.

## HIBERNATION

Some animals in cold climates escape the severest weather by hibernating. That is, they spend the winter months in a very long deep sleep. The word "hibernate" comes from the Latin *hibernare*, which means "to winter". Many animals find sheltered places underground or at the base of trees and hedges in which to hibernate.

Hibernating animals include frogs, newts, toads, lizards, dormice, bats, snails, tortoises, hedgehogs and squirrels. During hibernation the animal appears to be lifeless. Breathing almost stops and the heartbeat is slow. The feet, tails and snouts of warm-blooded animals are much colder than usual, although the blood in their hearts remains at a high temperature. The animals are nourished by sugars stored in the liver and by fat that has been built up during the summer.

Mild winters are bad for hibernating animals, because they wake up during warm spells, and use energy in moving about. But they do not feed normally and, by the end of the winter, are very thin.

Creatures which cannot burrow find cracks and holes in which to shelter. Some have been known to return to the same place year after year. Just as animals in cold climates escape winter by hibernating, so some in the tropics avoid hot, dry spells by sleeping underground. This is known as aestivation, from the Latin word meaning heat.

and newts called amphibia? **WHY** do cats purr?
**WHY** do some trees lose their leaves in winter?

## CATS PURR

Most people think that cats purr to show pleasure or contentment. Purring is a kind of low continous rattling hum, but it is nothing to do with a cat's real voice, for the vibration frequency is far lower than that of the vocal chords. In fact, a mother cat uses purring to call her kittens to feed. At birth kittens cannot see, hear or smell but they can feel the purring of their mother as a vibratory movement and so come towards it to nurse. Once the kittens are feeding, the mother stops purring. So it would seem that purring began as a kind of homing device and your cat may simply be reminding you that he is there so that you will continue to stroke him. On the other hand he is quite likely to give a sudden playful bite even when he is purring!

## TREES IN WINTER

Some trees with broad-bladed leaves lose their leaves in the winter because the tree has a rest period during the cold weather, and the leaves are not needed for the production of food. These trees are called deciduous trees— from the Latin *decidere* which means to fall. They drop their leaves in temperate or cold climates, but remain evergreen in the tropics.

Most of these trees grow in the deciduous belt of the earth. This is a mild, temperate region where the summers are warm and the winters cool, and rain falls throughout the year. Some also grow in tropical regions, and a few survive in sheltered places in the belt of the coniferous trees.

The fall of the leaves is brought about by the formation of a weak area, called the abscission layer, at the base of the leaf stalk or petiole. Before the leaves fall, the tree takes back some of the food in the leaves. Chemical changes take place. The result is the brilliant autumn colours of the leaves.

Scientists think that the shortening days in autumn have something to do with the formation of the abscission layer. As the hours of daylight lessen a zone of cells across the base of a leaf stalk softens until the leaf falls. A healing layer then forms on the stem and closes the wound. A leaf scar remains, which may be easily noticeable on winter twigs and help in identifying a tree.

In the spring the trees put forth their leaves and the cycle of nourishment begins again.

# WHY do birds eat grit? WHY do butterflies and moths have WHY are some

## BIRDS EAT GRIT

Birds which peck grain and other seeds also peck grit to help them to digest these hard foods. Because birds have no teeth, the work of chewing, which would require muscles and strong jaw bones, is done by the gizzard. This makes it possible for the skull to be delicate in structure and therefore light in weight.

Grit is taken into the gizzard, or ventriculus, which has thick and often very muscular walls and the combined action of the two grinds down the hard food. The ventriculus is the back part of a bird's stomach, the fore part is glandular and secretes digestive juices and is called the proventriculus. Food passes from the ventriculus to be absorbed by the intestines.

## BUTTERFLY WINGS

The "powder" on the wings of moths and butterflies is really a layer of tiny, coloured scales which overlap each other almost like the tiles on a roof. If you touch the wing with a finger the "powder" is rubbed off, leaving the wing more or less transparent and colourless.

The scales are generally like the shape of a hand tapered off at the wrist, and the whole surface is often grooved or cross-grooved. They are really hollow bags growing from tiny cup joints formed in the outer skin of the wing membranes.

They are either filled with colouring materials, or so minutely grooved and surfaced that they refract light to give off an irridescent colour, even though they contain no pigment. The brown, red, yellow, white or black scales are pigmented. The blues and greens are irridescent.

Many male butterflies and moths have specially shaped "scent-scales" (androconia). These are long and feather-like or broad and bat-shaped. They contain glands for making scents which attract the females.

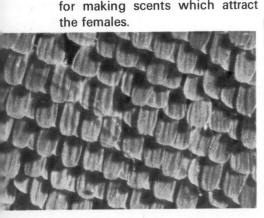

## MOTHS AND LIGHT

Moths are attracted to lights at night because they mistake them for the light of the moon which they use as a means of navigation. These other lights confuse the moths and make them lose their sense of direction.

In trying to keep the artificial light at the same angle as the moon's they circle it and come closer. Collectors use this behaviour to trap moths with a special electric bulb which gives off light rich in ultra-violet rays.

The insects are extremely responsive to these rays. But they cannot see red or yellow. So by using a red light you can watch them feeding at night without disturbing them.

## RABBITS' EARS

Rabbits are timid animals with many enemies and rely on their large ears to warn them of the sound of approaching danger. Their ears act like old-fashioned ear-trumpets. The large area catches a great many sound waves and channels them into the rabbit's inner ear.

Wild rabbits spend most of the day underground, usually coming out to feed between dusk and dawn. They are continually on the alert, their long ears twitching and moving round to pick up the faintest sound from an enemy. They also have a keen sense of smell.

Long back legs give rabbits speed. But they are virtually defenceless and, in fact, often seem to be hypnotized by approaching predators. When this happens, they crouch squealing and make no attempt to run away. Only their extraordinary fertility has enabled them to survive the onslaughts of foxes, badgers, wild cats, martens, stoats, weasels, polecats, dogs, man and disease.

The rabbit's close relative, the hare, has even longer ears. It, too, relies upon its acute hearing and sense of smell for warning. But it stands a good chance of escaping an enemy because its powerful hindquarters and unusually long back legs enable it to travel at an estimated speed of 40 miles an hour. A racing greyhound will gain on it eventually, but only after a long run, when the hare begins to tire.

# WHY do bats make a high-pitched sound as they fly? WHY
# WHY is the ichneumon fly known

## SOUND OF BATS

Bats use high-pitched sounds to find their way about. They are nocturnal animals. That is they move about by night. So they have developed their hearing to such an extent that they can find their way by a method known as echolocation.

The blind-flying abilities of bats were first studied by Lazzaro Spallanzani (1729–1799). He surgically removed the eyeballs from several bats to prove that they did not need to see to fly.

In the 20th Century, biologists, using electronic instruments, have carried out experiments with bats. They have discovered that bats find out where to go by emitting high-frequency sounds and receiving the echoes as they bounce off objects. Most of the sounds have too high a frequency to be heard by the human ear.

Bats commonly fly together in groups, but apparently they are not confused by the sounds and echoes produced by each other. When hunting in woods and in the rain they are able to discriminate between the faint echoes bouncing off insects and those bouncing off the ground, tree-trunks, branches, twigs and raindrops.

These tiny flying mammals have been using the equivalent of our modern sonar device for millions of years.

## SENSE OF SMELL

Dogs have a better sense of smell than we do because the physical structure of a dog is better adapted for scenting odours. In dogs this sense has remained keen, while in man it has become comparatively dull. Dogs use scent in feeding, detecting enemies, recognizing mates and offspring and in rivalry.

The chemical sense of smell is called chemoreception and the sense organs chemoreceptors. But there is little in the structure of the

## ICHNEUMON FLY

The Ichneumon fly is known as the farmer's friend because it controls a great many plant pests. Species have even been transported by man to colonize areas where artificial pest controls have not been successful.

Ichneumon flies, of which there are thousands of species spread throughout the world, are parasitic and their larvae feed on caterpillars, pupae and larvae of other insects.

Larva (plural, larvae) is the name given to an insect from the time it leaves the egg till it is transformed into the pupa or grub. The pupa (plural, pupae) is the name given to the chrysalis.

The female fly lays her eggs in or on the larvae or pupae of the host species. When the maggot-like parasitic larvae hatch out, they feed on the body fats and fluids of the host until they are fully grown. Then the parasitic larvae spin cocoons within which they pupate and from whence the adult fly emerges. In the case of parasitic larvae breeding inside the host, the latter behaves normally until shortly before the uninvited guest larva has fully developed.

There are some ichneumon flies which live on other ichneumon flies and these are called hyperparasitic. The different species of ichneumon vary greatly in size and the range extends from $\frac{1}{8}$" up to $1\frac{1}{2}$–2" in length.

# do dogs have a better sense of smell than we do?
## is the farmer's friend?    WHY   are birds' eggs so shaped?

nose to provide clues about its mechanism, and relatively little is known about how smell works. There are no accessory structures in the nose, and the receptors and nerve fibres leading to the brain are so fine that they are difficult to study. The chemoreceptors of human beings, dogs and other mammals lie in a cleft in each nostril.

During quiet breathing the main flow of air by-passes the cleft. But when a mammal sniffs, air is drawn into the clefts and over about half a square inch of yellowish tissue in which are embedded several million chemoreceptors. They are long thin cells with hair-like crowns making a web lying on the surface of the tissue which is bathed in mucus. These are connected to a part of the brain called the olfactory bulb, the size of which is a fair indication of the keeness of the sense of smell.

The olfactory bulb of a dog is much larger than that of a man. The moist nose of a dog also aids his sense of smell.

Smells are immensely important to dogs as we see from the way they refuse to by-pass a scent without investigating it and, very often, adding to it. They mark their home range and investigate passers-by. Their keen sense has been used by man as a help in hunting and tracking for many thousands of years.

## BIRDS' EGGS

The roundness of an egg allows pressure to be applied from the outside which would break it if applied from the inside. Thus a helpless chick is protected until the moment it needs to break out from its shell. It can then do this with the gentlest of tapping.

Eggs are hatched by an adult bird sitting on them, and the best container for round objects is a cup-shaped nest which prevents them rolling about. So the best shape for eggs is for one end to be smaller than the other. The normal position for eggs in a nest is to have the smaller ends pointing inwards. This means the eggs take up the minimum of room and make it easier for the sitting bird to cover them.

Birds with scanty nests, as in the case of most sea birds, have more elongated eggs. If such eggs are caught by the wind while lying on some cliff-face or rocky ledge, they will spin round instead of rolling over the edge.

# WHY do beavers build dams? WHY do fish have scales?

## BEAVERS

The beavers of North America build a dam to create an artificial lake in which to construct an island home or lodge. Often the beavers work in colonies. After choosing a narrow place in a shallow stream with a firm bottom, they set to work felling trees by standing on their hind legs and gnawing round the trunks with their large chisel-like teeth. When the tree is down, the beavers lop off the branches and cut the trunk into suitable lengths which they drag into the stream and sink across the current. Sticks, stones and mud are used to keep the dam in position and make it watertight.

In the middle of the lake thus created the beavers use the same materials to build their lodge. When completed this is a dome-shaped, ventilated structure about 8 feet in diameter and rising well clear of the surface of the lake. There are two entrances, both under water. One of these is used for general purposes, the other as an escape route in an emergency or for bringing in food.

The lodge serves as a home, a nursery for the baby beavers and a storehouse for food in winter. The beavers feed chiefly on the bark of trees, of which they keep a plentiful supply at the bottom of the dam, on the bed of the lake and built into the fabric of their home.

In winter, when the lake is frozen over and snow covers the ground, the lodge is virtually an impregnable fortress which the beavers can leave and enter by swimming under the ice. Beavers are experts at keeping the water in the lake at the right level by constructing canals. They work industriously to maintain both dam and lodge — hence the origin of that popular phrase about being "as busy as a beaver".

## FISH SCALES

Fish have scales as a protective coating for the skin. In fact, not all fish have them. But we usually think of a fish as a cold-blooded, aquatic animal that swims by means of fins, breathes by means of gills, and is covered with scales. Scales may be of four different kinds—placoid, ganoid, cycloid and ctenoid.

Placoid scales are long, spiny and toothlike, and are made of enamel and dentine. These are found on fishes which have a backbone made of gristle, such as sharks and rays.

Ganoid scales are rather like placoid scales but are mainly bony and covered with a kind of enamel called ganoin. These thick scales are found especially in garfish.

Cycloid scales are thin, large, round or oval scales arranged in an overlapping pattern. They are found in carps and similar fishes.

Ctenoid scales are similar to the cycloid ones, but have spines or comblike teeth along their free edges. These are found in the higher bony fishes, such as perches and sunfishes.

Scales are the remnants of the bony armour which enveloped the very earliest fish. Some fish such as lampreys and certain eels do not have scales.

# WHY do laurel and holly trees have shiny waxy leaves?

## LAUREL AND HOLLY

Laurel and holly trees have developed special kinds of leaves to seal the water inside them during the winter months.

Both trees are evergreen. Instead of dropping all their leaves in autumn, they shed old ones and grow new ones throughout the year. In winter the soil is too cold for the trees to draw water from it through their roots. Normal leaves would continue to transpire and to give off moisture until the trees died of drought. But the special leaves of the holly and laurel hold the water. Their waxy surface and leathery texture make certain that the water is contained safely within the green tissues.

Some of the holly leaves have a further modification. On the lower branches which are within reach of browsing animals, each leaf has a series of sharp points along its edge. The higher leaves have only a single point.

The leaves of the cherry laurel, if crushed, give out a faint but unmistakable smell of almonds because of the weak fumes of hydrocyanic (prussic) acid found in them. These fumes are poisonous. Scientists who want undamaged specimens of dead insects sometimes kill them by putting them with crushed laurel leaves in a closed glass tube.

## MENACE OF RABBITS

Rabbits became a menace in Australia because they breed so quickly and eat almost any vegetable. Three pairs of rabbits were introduced into Australia in the 18th Century. They multiplied so rapidly that, with the addition of others which were brought over, they spread over most of the continent and caused a tremendous amount of damage.

The female rabbit, or doe, produces four to eight litters of five to eight young in a year. They are blind, helpless and nearly naked at birth, but in two weeks are able to run, and in a month can fend for themselves. At the age of six months they are able to breed. It is reckoned that a pair of rabbits, given ideal conditions, could in three years have 13,718,000 descendants.

Many costly attempts to control the rabbits failed in Australia, but, in the early 1950s a virus disease called myxamatosis was introduced. The virus is a specific parasite of the rabbit and is transmitted by the mosquito and the rabbit flea. It is so lethal that 80 per cent of the rabbit population had died within three years. However, by 1960, a strain of rabbits resistant to the disease was again becoming a serious pest.

They cause an enormous amount of damage to Australian farmland. But the export of their skins has proved profitable, and Australia is a principal source of the rabbit fur used commercially.

# WHY were rabbits such a menace in Australia?
# WHY is the manchineel tree dangerous?

## MANCHINEEL

The manchineel tree is dangerous because its sap and fruit contain poison. Its other name is *Hippomane*, which comes from the Greek and means "causing horses to run mad".

The tree is a member of the Euphorbiaceae family and grows in tropical America, producing a crop of acrid, bitter apple-like fruits which drop spontaneously and carpet the ground beneath it. The sap is white and highly caustic, so that a drop on the skin produces a burning sensation and raises a blister. It used to be believed by many that to sleep beneath the tree meant certain death. But the great 18th Century naturalist Nicolas von Jacquin "reposed under it for hours at a time without inconvenience."

The wood has often been used for furniture as it is beautifully patterned in brown and white. Before felling the tree by hand, workmen light a fire round the trunk, so that the sap thickens and does not run down the handles of their axes.

32

WHY was Louis XIV known as the Sun King? WHY did the

# People and Events

## SUN KING

Louis XIV was the King of France from 1643 to 1715 and was known as the Sun King because of the general style and magnificence of his reign. Although he became king when he was four, he did not assume his full powers until 1661, after the death of the famous Cardinal Mazarin. Louis then became his own "first minister" and embarked upon years of personalized government.

Louis thoroughly enjoyed being king. He desired to shine in his role and a prime aim of his government was to foster any project that added to the king's glory.

He became a great patron of the arts and gave personal encouragement to writers who were to become some of the greatest names in French literature, including Molière and Racine.

Architecture, of course, was one of the most obvious ways of adding to the grandeur of his reign. The Palace of Versailles also took shape under his direction. He constantly changed his mind and frequently altered the plans for the palace. In 1685 Versailles, by then one of Europe's most beautiful palaces, became the Sun King's permanent seat of government. Louis entertained on an appropri-

ately lavish scale and the grace, elegance and excesses of his Court became a by-word throughout the civilized world. But he did have excellent taste. The delightful château of Marly-le-Roi is another example of this. Life at Court was governed by careful and meticulous rules, although the Sun King's love affairs were greatly resented by the nobility since his various mistresses were given high rank and exercised a considerable influence on policy. But despite Louis' very dubious private life he revelled in the title of "most Christian king" and did his best to protect the Catholic religion. This resulted in him making life for his Protestant subjects thoroughly uncomfortable. Indeed, in 1685 he issued an edict under which Protestantism was no longer tolerated in France. It is easy to smile at some of the Sun King's excesses but even Voltaire, the great French satirist, extolled his reign for the glory it added to the fame of France and French civilisation.

Louis encouraged good administration, promoted industry and attended diligently to his duties as "first minister" and steered France through the long war of the Spanish Succession.

## CIVIL WAR

The American Civil War (1861–65) arose chiefly over the question of Negro slavery. In the 15th Century the Portuguese found a ready market for Negro slaves, which they captured during their expeditions along the African coasts.

As the American continent developed, these slaves were eagerly sought to labour on the cotton and tobacco plantations, in mines, or in general farm work. Between 1680 and 1786 more than 2,000,000 slaves were transported and it was not until 1833 that the United Kingdom Parliament passed

# ...merican Civil War start?

an Act that set free all slaves in its territories.

In the United States the struggle between the slave-owning southern states and those of the North, where there was no slavery, was long and bitter. As the frontier moved westward, new states were seeking admission to the Union. Some had slaves and some did not.

In the north a growing party demanded immediate abolition of slavery, while in the south were some who threatened to leave the Union rather than give up their slaves. In 1860, Abraham Lincoln (1809—65) who favoured the gradual abolition of slavery, was elected President of the United States. Next year seven southern states left the Union and formed the Confederate States, with Jefferson Davis as president. On April 12, the officer in charge of Port Sumter, at Charleston, West Virginia, refused to surrender it to Confederate soldiers, who opened fire and thus began the Civil War.

Although the North had greater numbers, the South had better generals and the war dragged on for four years, with no fewer than 2,260 battles and skirmishes. In 1863, there were great victories for the North at Gettysburg and Vicksburg. It was at Gettysburg that Lincoln delivered his famous address promising freedom for all.

General Lee, commander of the Confederate armies, surrendered on April 9 at Appomatox Court House, Virginia.

*Detail from a painting of the Battle of Missionary Ridge, fought between November 23 and 25, 1863.*

34

WHY was Whitney's cotton gin important? WHY were

## WHITNEY'S GIN

Whitney's cotton gin was exceedingly important as it more than trebled the amount of cotton which could be picked free of seeds in a day. This stimulated the extension of the cotton plantations and the growth of Negro slavery in the south of the United States. In that way the cotton gin was indirectly responsible for the American Civil War.

Eli Whitney (1765–1825) was born in Westboro, Massachusetts. After graduating from Yale College in 1792, he became aware of the need for a machine which would separate cotton from its seeds. The Industrial Revolution was in full flood and inventions such as John Kay's flying shuttle (1733) and James Hargreaves's spinning jenny (1769) had created a growing demand for raw cotton as the production of finished goods was now so much faster and easier.

Whitney produced, in only a

few weeks, a hand-operated machine or gin, and by April 1793 had built a machine that could clean 50 pounds of cotton fibres a day. It consisted of a wooden cylinder encircled by rows of slender spikes, set half an inch apart, which extended between the bars of a grid set so closely together that the seeds could not pass, although the lint was pulled through by the revolving spikes. A revolving brush cleaned the spikes and the seeds fell into another compartment.

The gin was immediately in great demand. Country blacksmiths helped to fulfil the orders when the factory Whitney set up at New Haven, Connecticut, was unable to cope with all the orders. In the South, almost the whole region was given over to cotton growing, increasing the value of slaves and reinforcing the slave system, which had been declining.

## SLAVES

Negro slaves were taken to the West Indies because the original population had almost become extinct.

While Christopher Columbus explored all parts of the West Indies, his successors colonized only those islands which were peopled by the Ciboney and Arawak Indians. They avoided the Carib islands of the Lesser Antilles because they had no gold and the Carib Indians were fierce and difficult to subdue. As the Spaniards conquered each island, they rounded up its Indians and put

slaves taken to the West Indies?

them to work in mines or on plantations.

Many were worked to death, some starved, others died from diseases introduced from Europe and still others were killed when they tried to rebel. By 1550, the Ciboney were extinct and only a few Arawak remained.

In the 16th Century, the Spaniards introduced Negro slaves to replace the dwindling supply of labour. They did not bring in many, for their mines were exhausted, and they owned cattle ranches which did not require much labour.

The main shipments of Negro slaves came in the 18th Century, when sugar plantations were developed by the French in Haiti and the Lesser Antilles.

After the French Revolution, the slaves in Haiti revolted and set up an independent Negro republic. The French went to neighbouring British and Spanish islands, established new plantations and imported more slaves. ●

When slavery was abolished in the first half of the 19th Century the British imported Chinese and Indians from Asia who rapidly

*An interior view of a House of Correction in Jamaica in the 1830s. The whipping of female slaves was a commonplace cruelty. This contemporary print illustrated an anti-slavery pamphlet.*

increased in numbers until, by the middle of the 20th Century, they comprised more than one third of the population of Trinidad. Throughout the Antilles the Negroes and Asians have assumed more and more prominence, so that they now dominate the area except in countries like Cuba and Puerto Rico.

# WHY was the Great Wall of China built?        WHY did the

## GREAT WALL

The Great Wall of China was built in the Third Century BC to keep out the raiding Tartars of Mongolia. It is 20 to 30 feet high and 15 to 25 feet wide at the top, with towers 60 feet high every few hundred yards.

The Wall stretches from Shanhaikwan on the Yellow Sea to the borders of Kansu and Sinkiang in the west, crossing high mountains and deep valleys. Probably over 500,000 workers were employed to build it. Even today, the Wall is in a wonderful state of preservation.

This marvellous structure is constructed of brick and stone. The sides have battlements—parapets with openings or embrasures through which weapons could be discharged.

All large cities of China were provided with similar walls, and the gates were closed at night to give the citizens protection against surprise attack. For China has been envied by her neighbours throughout history. Many times these neighbours have invaded the country, seized the capital and begun a new dynasty.

*Probably man's greatest-ever constructional achievement. More than 500,000 workers were employed to build it.*

# Roman Civilization fall?

## ROMAN CIVILIZATION

Rome's conquest of the Near East, mainly in the last century B.C. probably sowed the seeds of decay which led to the fall of one of the mightiest empires ever known.

Beginning as a tiny settlement on the Palatine Hill, about 17 miles from the mouth of the Tiber in central Italy, Rome had become the conqueror and leader of the Western world.

But then the ancient and sturdy simplicity of the Roman character gave way to Oriental luxury and bitter hostility developed between the wealthy aristocracy and the poverty stricken majority.

The death of Tiberius Gracchus in 133 B.C. marked the beginning of a century of revolution and civil war which ended in the downfall of the republic and the establishment of an empire. Julius Caesar

(102–44 B.C.), the great warrior-statesman, welded the tottering structure together and two centuries of peace followed. They included periods of great splendour, such as the wise rule of Hadrian (A.D. 117–138), when the empire reached its greatest extent.

The Christian religion spread until, in the reign of Constantine (280–337), it become the official faith of the Roman Empire. Rome was prosperous and her influence in art and letters reigned throughout the known world, but prosperity brought corruption and self-indulgence completed the ruin.

Diocletian (284–305) took the first step which led to the division of the empire, entrusting an associate with the government of the west, while he ruled the east. Then Constantine the Great in 330 moved the capital to the Greek city of Byzantium, renaming it Constantinople.

The story of the Byzantine Empire is long and glorious but that of the western empire is one of weakness and decline. Northern barbarians invaded Italy and in 410 the Visigoth King Alaric conquered Rome. The western empire from that time became the prey of successive waves of fierce barbarians.

In 476 Romulus Augustus, the last of the imperial line in the west, was deposed by the barbarian leader Odoacer, and the Roman Empire was formally ended.

However, in reading the history of France, Italy and Spain, you will see that the end of the Roman Empire was in a way only its beginning. These new kingdoms governed themselves mainly by Roman law, spoke forms of Latin and professed the Christian religion. Thus even though a great empire decayed and fell, Rome had won a dominion which persists to this day.

# WHY do some countries have colonies?    WHY is Texas

## COLONIES

Some countries still have colonies and dependencies because these are usually small territories, often with few inhabitants, which do not have the capacity to carry out all those aspects of administration and government necessary to an independent state.

Nowadays, the possession of colonies is an embarrassment rather than an advantage to the country having them, and few are retained against the wishes of their people. Before the great decolonising years which followed the Second World War, having colonies seemed a natural part of being a great power.

France had many overseas territories such as Algeria, French Morocco and those of French West Africa, but all of these are now self-governing republics. Italy had Eritrea, now federated with Ethiopia, and Italian Somaliland, now the Somali Democratic Republic. Holland's old Dutch East Indies is mostly the present-day Republic of Indonesia.

As in the case of the British Empire the breaking up of these empires left many small territories who were not big enough for independence or who preferred to wait. These saw advantages in remaining under the protective umbrella of a greater power.

Such protection means that defence, external affairs, internal security, and the safeguarding of the terms and conditions of public officers is the responsibility of the colonizing power through its appointed governor.

In some cases the governor is also responsible for the financial and economic stability of the territory. But internal affairs are normally in the hands of the locals.

## LONE STAR STATE

Texas is called the 'Lone Star State' because for almost ten years, from 1836 until its annexation by the United States in 1845, the country was independent.

For three centuries up to 1821, Texas and Mexico had belonged to Spain. In all that time, Spain had shown hardly any interest in this vast territory which is equal in size to the total area of France, Belgium, the Netherlands and Denmark combined. When Mexico gained her independence, Texas was peopled by no more than 7,000 and with only three settlements large enough to be called towns. Beset with her own problems of administration and revolts, Mexico allowed American families to colonize land in Texas.

By 1835 there were around 30,000 Americans settled in Texas, outnumbering the Mexicans by four to one. Too late for her own interests, Mexico tried to discipline the American Texans by abolishing slavery, levying duties and establishing military garrisons. Fighting broke out when martial law was declared by the Mexicans who tried to disarm the Texans. On October 2, 1835, the Texans won the first battle of the Texas revolution at Gonzales. San Antonio was captured in December and the Mexicans withdrew to Mexico.

The Texans were weakened by arguments and lack of unity which allowed the Mexicans to recapture San Antonio on March 2, 1836, but while the Mexicans closed in on the Alamo, Texas declared her independence. The new nation found this independence difficult to manage and was relieved to be annexed in 1845 by a rather unwilling United States of America.

called "the Lone Star State"?

**WHY** did the Vietnam War occur?

## VIETNAM WAR

The Vietnam War had its roots firmly established in the authoritarian colonial rule of the French which was formally recognized at the Convention of Tientsin in May 1885. The name Vietnam came into Western use in 1946 to designate the eastern part of Indochina stretching from the borders of China in the north to the delta of the Mekong River in the south. French colonial rule generated a deep dissatisfaction among the Vietnamese, and the Indochinese Communist Party, formed by Ho Chi Minh, arose in 1930.

During the Second World War, the Japanese worked with the French to suppress rebellion. But, in 1941 Ho Chi Minh established the Vietnam League for Independence, generally known as the Viet Minh, which, after Japan's surrender, seized control of Hanoi, in the North, and proclaimed Vietnam's independence.

The French attempted to reassert their rule in the Franco-Vietnamese War (1946–54) but were unsuccessful, even with generous financial help from the United States. An international conference at Geneva in 1954 under the co-chairmanship of Brittain and Russia, with China and United States playing major roles, divided the country into two at the 17th parallel, with the Communist Viet Minh in the North and French forces in the South.

After the settlement, the United States undertook to build a separate anti-Communist state in the South, with Ngo Dinh Diem as Prime Minister at Saigon. However, his rule became increasingly unpopular and a Communist People's Revolutionary Party (Viet Cong) was established in 1962, pledged to bring communism to South Vietnam.

Diem was overthrown and killed, and after three other short-lived governments, President Nguyen Van Thieu assumed control. Viet Cong estimated military strength rose rapidly and the United States began to move military advisers into the country. In 1965 America began bombing raids on the north and introduced the first contingent of United States marines.

The country was locked in a bitter struggle in which the Viet Minh and Viet Cong maintained their offensive despite the vast number of men, money and resources poured into Vietnam by the United States of America.

## TAJ MAHAL

The Taj Mahal was built by the Mogul emperor Shah Jehan (1614–66) as a tomb for his favourite wife, Mumtaz Mahal. It is situated at Agra in northern India and is one of the most beautiful buildings in the world. When the Moguls arrived in India early in the 16th Century, they brought Persian civilization with them. The tomb is a perfect example of the Persian style of architecture.

The name of the tomb means "Crown of the Palace", one of the titles given to the Empress Mumtaz. It is built of white marble, inlaid with precious stones, and is eight-sided, 130 feet across at its widest points and nearly 200 feet high to the top of the huge dome. It is flanked on each side by two slender minarets and stands on a vast marble terrace overlooking the River Jumna and surrounded by Persian gardens.

Inside, under the dome, are the marble cenotaphs or monuments of Shah Jehan and his empress, on which the sun flickers through marble screens as delicate and intricate as lace. The walls are covered in floral designs and inscriptions from the Koran, picked out in onyx, jasper, cornelian and other semi-precious stones. The tombs which hold the royal bodies are in a vaulted chamber below and, in contrast to the chamber itself, are quite plain.

According to a legend the marvellous building appeared to Mumtaz in a dream and the Shah searched the whole of India for an architect. The plans were said to have been drawn up only after the architect had been given a drug which enabled him to see a vision of the monument in all its splendour and glory.

## DICTATORS

We call a dictator "benevolent" if he uses his powers for the good of the people, not simply for his own. The word "benevolent" is derived from the Latin and means "well-wishing", but though many dictators have promised to defend the rights of the populace, most of them have failed to do so.

A dictator is a ruler who, usually because of some emergency, is given extraordinary powers of government. The office was first instituted in ancient Rome in 501 B.C. to deal with serious military, civil or criminal disturbances. The dictator was described as the "administrative dictator" (*rei gerundae causa*) and held office for six months. The time limit was intended to ensure that some of these dictators were benevolent.

Modern dictators, like the ancient ones, have taken over the reins of government in times of crisis, but they have used their powers to establish a permanent and often tyrannical rule. Both Benito Mussolini and Adolph Hitler eventually became heads of government formally, in accordance with the constitution. Present day dictatorships include the long established figure of Spain's General Franco and more recently Uganda's President Amin.

Perhaps the best example of a benevolent dictator is Napoleon Bonaparte (1769–1821), Napoleon I of France from 1804 to 1814 and again for the "Hundred Days" in 1815. He seized absolute power in France, but his ambitions were for his country and his people rather than for himself. Under his rule industry expanded and the universities flourished, while he left enduring legacies in the shape of the Code Napoleon (the codification of French civil law), the reorganization of the judicial system, the Bank of France and the establishment of the military academies such as St. Cyr.

called ''benevolent''?

## AMERICA

America gets its name from the traditional family name Amerigo belonging to Amerigo Vespucci (1454–1512), who was an Italian navigator and merchant.

Vespucci began his career in the bank of Lorenzo and Giovanni Pier Francesco de' Medici. In 1491, he was sent to Seville, where he met Columbus. At the beginning of 1505 he was summoned to the court of Spain for a private consultation and was appointed chief navigator for the famous Casa de Contración de las Indias (Commercial House for the West Indies), a post of great responsibility, which he held until his death.

The period during which he made his voyages falls between 1497 and 1504. The first took place in 1499–1500 when, it is believed, he discovered the mouth of the Amazon and sailed as far as the Cape of La Consolación or São Agostinho (about 6° latitude South). On the way back he reached Trinidad and then made for Haiti, believing all the time that he was sailing along the coast of the extreme easterly peninsula of Asia.

At the end of 1500, under the auspices of the Portuguese government, he reached the coast of Brazil and discovered the Plate river. This voyage was of tremendous importance in that Vespucci became convinced, and convinced others, that the newly discovered lands were not part of Asia, but a New World.

In 1507, a humanist scholar named Waldseemüller suggested that the newly discovered world should be named America, after Amerigo. The extension of the name to North America came later. The first official use of the name United States of America was in the Declaration of Independence of 1776.

## ASSASSINS

Some murderers are called assassins because this name was given in the 11th Century to a sect of Shi'ite Muslim fanatics who pledged themselves to murder those who did not believe in their religion.

The word assassin comes from the Arab *hashishi* or hashish eater, supposedly because the killers were alleged to take hashish to give ecstatic visions of paradise before setting out on a mission which might well end in their own deaths. We use the word now for one who kills a public figure.

The history of the Shi'ite Muslim sect began in 1090 in Persia, where it was founded by Hassan ibn al-Sabbah and where its endeavours were chiefly directed against the regime of the Seljuks, a Turkish family who had invaded western Asia and founded a powerful empire.

In the 12th Century the assassins extended their activities to Syria, where the expansion of Seljuk rule and the arrival of the Christian crusaders gave them ample scope. They seized a group of castles and waged a war of terror against rulers and crusaders. At one time, they made a pact with Saladin (1138–1193) and murdered Conrad de Montferrat, a crusader who had been made King of Jerusalem. The successive assassin chiefs in Syria were known as the "Old Man of the Mountain". The chief of the sect in Persia proclaimed himself as ruler or Imam.

The end of the power of the assassins came in the 13th Century. The last of their castles fell in 1272. There are still followers of the sect to be found in Syria, Iran and Pakistan, where they are known as Khojas.

Today they owe allegiance to the Aga Khan, as the spiritual leader of the Nizari Isma'ili sect of the Shi'ite Mohammedans.

# called assassins? WHY are some soldiers called mercenaries?

*A mercenary cleans his gun on the shores of the Congo River near Stanleyville.*

## MERCENARIES

Mercenaries are soldiers who give their services, and, if necessary, their lives, to anyone who will pay them enough to do so. They were common even in ancient times.

Sometimes they were slaves, as were the Nubians who served the first Pharaohs, or freebooters, such as the Philistines who were found in armies throughout the ancient Near East.

In mediaeval armies, professional soldiers often went to war instead of vassals who owed allegiance to a king or noble. The vassal had to furnish a certain number of armed men to fight in his lord's service for 40 days a year, but an alternative levy of gold was permitted which was used to hire mercenaries.

Mercenaries dominated the turbulent period from the Black Death of the mid-14th Century to the end of the wars of religion three centuries later. The bands which devastated France in the Hundred Years' War (1337–1453) were like those which ruined Germany in the Thirty Years' War (1618–48). The wealthy cities of Renaissance Italy gave them long-term contracts for they were tough, skilful men who could cope with any kind of disturbance.

There are still men whose love of adventure and action leads them to enlist with any army who will pay them enough. Many governments, especially those in developing nations, are anxious to pay for their daring and expertise.

Through the ages mercenaries have become heroes, murderers, and the inevitable face of war.

# WHY were the pyramids built?

## PYRAMIDS

Pyramids are found both in the old world and the new. We associate the name pyramid with the colossal tombs in Egypt, but there are many more in central America which were erected by the Aztecs as altars to their gods.

The royal tombs of ancient Egypt are situated on the west bank of the Nile, near Memphis. The best examples are the three great pyramids of Gizeh, probably built between 2690 and 2560 BC. The largest, the Great Pyramid, was erected by King Khufu (Cheops) and its base covers an area of 13 acres.

Great skill was displayed in planning and laying out the pyramids. Stones were transported across the Nile from quarries on the east side. The sides of the pyramid were faced to the cardinal points (the four points of the compass), and the base was nearly a perfect square.

An immense amount of slave labour was needed to raise the vast structures, with the blocks being hauled along sloping ramps.

Stonecutters and masons used saws up to nine feet long.

The pyramids were designed to protect the mummies of kings and queens and the vast treasure buried with them. The polished granite and limestone slabs which once encased their sides have been removed, but the complicated interior passages and chambers, composed of rough-hewn blocks of stone or brickwork still remain. However, tomb-robbers were busy even in the time of the pharaohs, and no pyramid has preserved its treasures intact.

The Aztec pyramids were the scenes of human sacrifice, the victims being led one by one up the steep steps of the pyramid and stretched out on a humped stone by four black-robed priests. A fifth priest ripped open their chests with a stone knife and tore out their hearts. These were burnt in a stone vessel, as nourishment for the gods. The bodies were thrown down the pyramid, near the base of which was a great rack full of the skulls of previous victims.

46

# WHY is fascism considered evil?   WHY is South America

*The march on Rome — Mussolini is the third from the left.*

## EVIL OF FASCISM

Fascism is considered evil by those nations who believe strongly in personal liberty, on the grounds that it disregards individual rights, as well as humanity, in its exclusive concern for the nation. Fascism is a political attitude which sees the authority of the nation, state or race as the centre of life. The Italian word *fascismo* comes from the Latin *fasces* (bundles) which described the bundle of rods with an axe which was the symbol of the law's authority in ancient Rome.

As founded in Italy in 1919 by Benito Mussolini (1883–1945), fascism proclaimed its intention to create order out of chaos and replace argument with decision. In fact, it established an authoritarian regime by violence, dictated unity and gave overall priority to military discipline, fighting spirit and ruthless action. Fascism insisted on the ''iron logic of nature'' that the weak would be conquered by the strong. War was regarded as inevitable. So the chief aim was to make the nation strong and resolute. Mussolini said: ''War is to the man what maternity is to the woman''.

In fascism service to the nation is the one supreme duty. Absolute devotion is instilled into all citizens by the use of all means of communication. Criticism of the government is not allowed. Cultural or intellectual exchange with other countries is closely regulated. During the 1930s the movement became world-wide with Germany quickly gaining the ascendancy, and Austria, Hungary, Poland, Romania, Bulgaria and Japan joining the ranks.

In Spain the civil war ended in 1939 with the victory of the fascist General Franco. The Second World War resulted in defeat for fascism, but fascist ideas succeeded in surviving in some countries and reviving in others.

argely Roman Catholic?

## ROMAN CATHOLIC

South America is largely Roman Catholic because the continent was first discovered and opened up by explorers from the strongly Roman Catholic countries of Spain and Portugal.

Venezuela was the first of the South American countries to be colonized by the Spaniards. Christopher Columbus discovered it on his third voyage in 1498, and settlers soon followed in the early 16th Century. Uruguay, discovered by the Spanish explorer, Juan Diaz de Solis, in 1515, was claimed over the years—until its independence in 1830—by both the Portuguese in Brazil and the Spanish in Argentina. Brazil, although first discovered by a Spaniard in 1500,

was declared a possession of the Portuguese crown in the same year by Pedro Alvares Cabral.

In the early 16th Century, Colombia and Ecuador were also conquered by the Spanish. In 1532, Francisco Pizarro added to the Spanish dominions by the conquest of Peru and its Inca empire, which at that time included much of what is now Bolivia, Chile, Columbia and Ecuador.

Paraguay was claimed for Spain by Sebastian Cabot in 1526. The Spanish captain, Pedro de Mendoza, established a settlement on the site of what is now Buenos Aires in 1536. Although this was soon burnt down by Indians, Juan

de Garay and other Spanish settlers reestablished the settlement in 1580 and gave it the name Santos Trinidad y Puerto de Santa Maria de Buenos Aires. This long name which means Holy Trinity and Harbour of Our Lady of Kind Winds, was soon shortened to Buenos Aires.

This history of the Spanish and Portuguese control in South America is one of oppression and exploitation. In the early 19th Century, the colonies revolted and established republics. One of the strongest forces remaining from the centuries of colonial domination is the vital Roman Catholic faith of the conquistadores—the conquerors.

# WHY is Paul Revere famous?   WHY did the British Empire

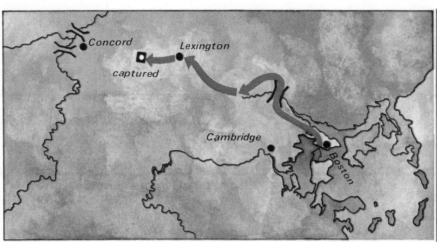
*Paul Revere's ride*

## PAUL REVERE

Paul Revere (1735–1818) is famous for his ride on horseback during the American Revolution to warn Massachusetts colonists of the approach of British troops.

Paul Revere's father, a Huguenot refugee, who had settled in Boston, Massachusetts, taught his son the art of silversmithing. Revere became a great artist in silver but, in his need to support his family he also sold spectacles, replaced missing teeth and made surgical instruments.

He was a fervent patriot, cut many copper plates for anti-British propaganda and was a leader of the Boston Tea Party in 1773, when a group of citizens disguised as Indians threw a cargo of tea into the sea as a protest against the British tax on it.

In 1775, when the American Revolution broke out, Revere constructed a powder mill to supply the colonial troops. He enlisted in the army and in 1776 was a lieutenant-colonel, in command of Castle William, at Boston.

But his most famous exploit took place the year before when, as principal express rider for Boston's Committee of Safety, he warned Middlesex County, on April 18, that British troops were leaving Boston to seize military stores at Lexington and Concord. His exploit has been immortalized in the poem *Paul Revere's Ride* by Henry Wadsworth Longfellow (1807–1882).

After the colonists' victory, Revere set up a rolling mill for the manufacture of sheet copper in Massachusetts, and became rich.

## BRITISH EMPIRE

It is possible to list at least four basic forces which brought about the dissolution of the British Empire. First, both Britain and her colonies recognized that some kind of self-government was necessary in territories which were separated by thousands of miles from Britain. Administration centred in London was increasingly difficult and expensive.

Secondly, the colonies themselves began to chafe against British rule and to demand to manage their own affairs. A note of aggressive nationalism entered into the appeals for self-government.

In the third place, individual British colonies and other nations began to forge economic, social and political links. Two world wars also greatly reduced Britain's power in the world and made some colonies look elsewhere for leadership.

Finally, many Britons themselves realized that the Empire had

## MING VASE

Ming porcelain is admired and distinguished for its use of colour. It was the most important development of China's Ming Dynasty (1368–1644) in the realms of art. A completely new style arose in which the emphasis was on the decorative element as opposed to form and glaze with which the potters of the Sung (960–1279) and Yüan (1280–1368) dynasties had been concerned.

During the Ming dynasty production of Chinese porcelain reached a very high standard. This was especially so in the case of the imperial porcelain factory at Ching-tê Chên which had ample deposits of the finest white clay to draw upon. Chinese fashion at this period turned towards richness of colouring and to striking effects in decoration. The full-bodied sturdy shapes and the gorgeous colouring of Ming porcelain reflected the prosperous community which produced it.

There were three methods employed by the potters to create the colourful decorations. One, used in the T'ang dynasty (618–906), was to scratch a line which, as well as strengthening the design, form

become unwieldy and that relationships within it were a handicap rather than a gain.

Nevertheless, there was not a complete break up but the growth of an association of independent nations called the Commonwealth. There were three bonds which united the association. The close economic relationship of trade, labour and capital; the acceptance of many Commonwealth countries of British social, economic, educational, political, military and legal institutions and customs and the savings that could be made in the member countries by acceptance of British military and diplomatic services.

## ...OWER

...flower sailed to America ...ort the Pilgrim Fathers ...and to Plymouth, Massa- ...where they established ...ermanent colony in New ...n 1620.

...of the Pilgrims were ...of a separatist group ...Church of England, who, ...f religious persecution, ...d first to Leiden in Hol- ...life in Holland was hard, ...eparatists and 65 others, ...group from England be- ...mostly to the Anglican ...et sail for America.

...ayflower was a square- ...ailing ship which had ...carried wine and was ...ith 12 cannon. Among the ...n board were John Carver, ...Bradford and Captain ...tandish, who had been ...his military knowledge.

...ip sailed from Southamp- ...land, on August 15, 1620 ...passengers and soon ran ...ce storms which necessi-

tated some repairs. The voyage lasted 66 days. One child—a boy— was born to Elizabeth Hopkins at sea. Another was born on board to Susanna White as the ship lay at anchor off Cape Cod.

At Cape Cod the Pilgrims drew up a covenant, now known as the Mayflower Compact, which bound them to obey the government which should be set up. Within 10 years the colony was prosper- ous and expanding, and was able to dissolve the financial partner- ship it had made with merchants back in England. The first settlers did not become known as the Pilgrim Fathers until two cenuries after their arrival when Daniel Webster made a speech beginning: "We have come to record here our homage to our Pilgrim Fathers . . ."

Little is known of the Mayflower after her epic voyage, but it is said that her timbers were used to build the barn at the old Jordans Hostel at Jordans in Buckinghamshire, England.

*...ruction of The Mayflower set sail for America in 1957.*

## DEMOCRACY

Democracy is considered good because it recognizes the rights of the individual and strives to maintain and protect those rights, for instance freedom of speech and religion.

The word democracy comes from the Greek "demokration", from "demos", the people, and "kratos", rule. The concept of rule by the people for the people un- doubtedly goes back to prehistoric times but, in western political tradition, we associate it with the city-states of ancient Greece.

There it was a form of govern- ment known as direct democracy. Decisions were made by the whole body of citizens, acting under the procedure of majority rule. How- ever, we must remember that not everyone was a citizen. Women were not allowed to vote and there were many slaves who had no rights at all.

It is easy to see how difficult this system would be to organize in a large country and indeed there

## BOTANY BAY

Botany Bay became famous as the place in Australia to which English convicts were transported after Captain James Cook had taken possession of the continent for Britain in 1770.

Cook sailed up to Botany Bay, near the site of the present city of Sydney, and named the continent New South Wales, because he thought its coastline resembled that of South Wales. Botany Bay was so called by Joseph Banks, a botanist in Cook's expedition, be- cause of the bay's rich plant life.

Until then Britain had trans- ported most of her convicts to work on the American plantations. But when the North American colonies gained their indepen- dence in 1782, it was decided to send the convicts to Australia, chiefly because of the great dis- tance.

break up? WHY is a Ming vase so admired? WHY

50

ed a ditch to separate the various fields of colour. A second method was to separate these areas by putting down tiny raised borders to these fields by means of threads of clay. Then a third way was to create the design in relief, so that it was easy to separate the colours for the raised decoration from those for the background.

Towards the close of the Ming period, the standard of pottery declined and it came to succeedi 1912) th again flo

*This magnificent vase was found i*

# onsidered good? WHY was Botany Bay famous?
# WHY is Mao Tse-tung so powerful?

was a gap of about 2,000 years before the idea of representative democracy arose. This is a form of government where the citizens exercise the same rights as in direct democracy, but through representatives chosen by and responsible to them.

Nowadays, most countries in the world are democracies, in name at least. That is, they claim a form of government, elected by the people, whose powers are limited by a constitution. Theoretically this means that although the majority are in power, they are bound by law to guarantee individual and collective rights to those who are in the minority. But in many countries theory does not always conform with practice.

We also use the word democratic to describe any political or social system which is attempting to bring about equality among the people, especially in the distribution of private property.

In January 1788, a fleet of nine transports carrying 828 convicts, of whom 300 were women, and escorted by two warships, arrived in Botany Bay. Captain Authur Philip (1735–1814) who was in charge of the expedition and was appointed governor, established a settlement which he called Sidney, after Lord Sidney (1733–1800) who was British Colonial Secretary.

The colony became a dumping ground for the rejects of Britain but many of those transported were guilty only of small offences. Some free men also settled there, and the convicts worked as unpaid servants to the officials and free settlers. Even when they had served their sentences, most preferred to remain in Australia, where they were given grants of land, and helped to build a colony.

## MAO TSE-TUNG

Mao Tse-tung the Communist party leader and founder of the modern Republic of China is virtually dictator of his country, with control over all mass media and education. The vast majority of the hundreds of millions of Chinese regard him with almost reverential awe as the symbol of a better way of life. The Ninth Party Congress of April 1969 confirmed Mao's leadership as well as his choice of a successor as articles of the party constitution. Every loyal Chinese Communist regards the *Political Thoughts of Mao Tse-tung* with reverence.

Mao Tse-tung was born in 1893 into a moderately prosperous peasant family in the central Chinese province of Hunan. He was a restless young man who attended school after school and embraced creed after creed until he finally found his faith in Marxism and made revolution his career.

He was quick to realize the hidden power of the peasants, organized them for action and gradually gained control of the Chinese Communist Party which he had first shared with a Soviet-trained group of leaders.

The Chinese war with Japan (1937–45) forced Mao Tse-tung into an uneasy alliance with the Nationalist Party (Kuomintang) under Chiang Kai-shek. After that war ended with Japan's defeat, civil war broke out (1946–49) ending in victory for the Communists and the defeat of Chiang Kai-shek who fled to Taiwan. The Nationalist capital was declared at T'ai-pei, while Mao proclaimed a people's republic on the mainland with himself as chairman. After Stalin's death in 1953, Mao gradually turned away from the Soviet Union and an open break developed between the two countries in the early 1960s.

# Geography and the Earth

## ABU SIMBEL

When construction began on the High Dam at Aswan, in southern Egypt, it was realized that the temples of Abu Simbel would be completely submerged as the waters of the Nile rose behind the dam to create a much needed reservoir.

In 1959 Egypt, and its southern neighbour Sudan appealed for help to the United Nations Educational, Scientific and Cultural Organization. The first archeological surveys began in 1960 and U.N.E.S.C.O's response grew into what was to become the biggest archaeological rescue operation in history.

Abu Simbel consists of three temples of Rameses II built more than 3,000 years ago. The most important and impressive temple included four gigantic seated statues of the king, each 65 feet high. By 1968 these four enormous monuments to Rameses had been cut out of the rock and reconstructed, exactly as they were, high up on a cliff.

Six more great statues of Rameses and his queen (about 30 feet high) were also excavated and moved to a dry sanctuary above the old river bed, along with everything else that could be salvaged.

# Mercator's projection important to geographers?

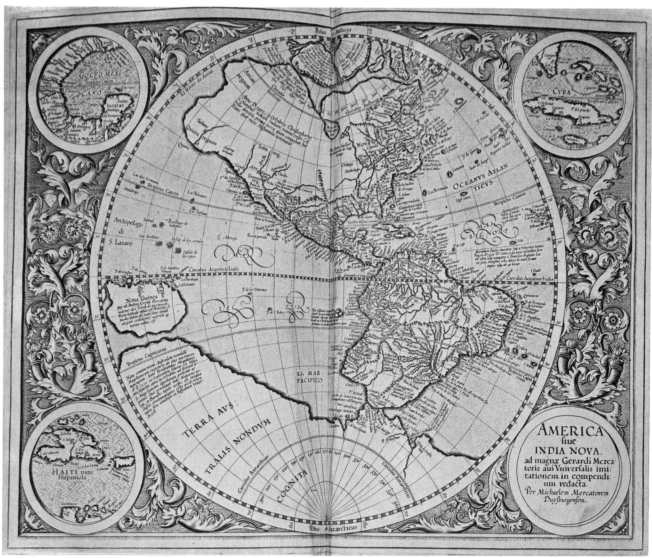

*Mercator's original projection*

## MERCATOR

Gerardus Mercator's (1512–94) projection is important to geographers because, unlike other projections, a straight line drawn on it gives a true compass bearing.

A projection is simply a means of transferring a round section of the world on to a flat sheet of paper. This is more easily said than done, for, no matter how hard you try, you cannot do it without altering the shapes or sizes of countries or the distances between them.

You can try this for yourself. Draw a rough map of the world on an orange with a felt tip pen, then cut the orange into sections. When you have eaten the orange, try to arrange the curved pieces of peel into a flat map. You can see that if the lands by the Equator, or the widest parts of the orange peel, are touching, there are large gaps to the north and south. To make a map in which there are no gaps, it is necessary to stretch these lands in the north and south—and this is just what Mercator did.

The history of projections goes back to the Greeks who realized as long ago as 500 B.C. that the world was round. Eratosthenes, a Greek who lived at Alexandria in the Second Century B.C. even calculated the circumference of the world to be 25,000 miles. His estimate was only a little more than the correct distance which is 24,901·8 miles at the Equator.

Mercator's projection increases the distances between the lines of latitude (the lines parallel to the Equator) as one moves further north or south. While this makes the map useful for navigation, it also gives people many wrong ideas about the world. It makes some countries, such as Greenland, appear too large. The areas of land at the Equator on Mercator's projection are correct. But those at 45° North or South are doubled, and those at 75° are nearly 16 times too large.

# WHY do deserts form? WHY are igneous rocks different from WHY are there locks on some canals and rivers?

## DESERTS

Deserts in hot climates owe their origin to lack of water resulting from the capacity of warm air above the desert area to retain most of the available moisture. This, combined with the high evaporation rate, turn the land into desert.

Another factor in the formation of deserts is a high mountain range, such as the Andes. These enormous mountains lie across the path of the rain clouds and moist winds, thus forming a shield. So most of the rain clouds burst over the mountains before they ever reach the plains. Other deserts, such as the Gobi in Central China, are so deep within the continent that the moisture-laden winds hardly ever reach them.

## IGNEOUS ROCKS

Sedimentary rocks are formed from the sediment, or broken pieces of the earth's rock structure worn down by weather and erosion. The fragmented pieces become compacted and in time much of it is cemented in to form rock.

Igneous rocks originate either from volcanic action as molten lava, which hardens, or from the slow cooling of molten masses beneath the earth's surface, which are exposed after a volcanic eruption or after much erosion.

Many important minerals, notably uranium, have been found enveloped in igneous rocks. The chief sedimentary rocks are sandstone, shale, dolomite and limestone.

## RIVER DELTAS

A river winding its way down to the sea, from its mountain source, will inevitably choose the lowest land through which to flow. By the time the river approaches the sea the speed at which it is travelling will have decreased considerably, thus allowing the water to drop its load of sediment and other solids.

These solid particles (alluvium), therefore, form the land pockets which are characteristic of the various branches of a river delta. Owing to slow pace of a river at this stage, it will wind its way round any elevated land points rather than go over them.

Deltas are most likely to form

where the sea, into which the river flows, is particularly calm for most of the year. Notable deltas in the world include the Mississippi (the largest) the Ganges, and the Nile. A delta is so called because it is the name of the fourth letter of the Greek alphabet whose shape it resembles.

sedimentary rocks? WHY do river deltas form?
WHY does the Sahara constantly change shape?

## SAHARA

The Sahara, the world's greatest dry hot desert, stretches right across the north of Africa where there is almost no rainfall and, consequently, little or no vegetation to anchor the soil. The sand is blown constantly by the wind, much of it into a landscape of great shifting dunes which constantly change shape, while the edges of the desert eternally encroach upon the land around.

The Sahara extends over three and a half million square miles of and, where the average rainfall is generally much less than 10 inches a year. The prevailing winds come from the heart of Asia and carry little moisture.

The temperature during the day exceeds 100°F. in the summer, and even in the winter averages 60°–70°F. The surface of the sand is sometimes as hot as 170°F. The sun beats down from a clear sky all day, but at night the same cloudless sky allows the land to cool quickly, and there is often frost at dawn in winter.

The wind acts as a great sand-blasting machine, constantly wearing down rocks and carrying sand and small pebbles along. The few desert plants survive because they have long roots or thick fleshy leaves, and stems that reduce water loss and may even store moisture.

A desert oasis is simply a place where there is water. The greatest oasis of all is Egypt, where for thousands of years life has depended on the careful use of the waters of the River Nile.

## CANAL LOCKS

Locks are watertight chambers which enable boats to ascend or descend to different levels in a canal or river.

The lock is usually rectangular in shape with gates at either end. If a boat has to go to a higher level it enters through the bottom or downstream gates of the lock, which are then closed. The water level in the lock is raised to that of the higher part of the canal by filling from the upper level and the upstream gates are opened to let the boat out. The opposite procedure takes place when a boat needs to descend.

Locks used to be made of timber, brick or stone, but now concrete and steel piling are more usual. Originally the chamber was filled or emptied by sluices in the gates. Nowadays, as locks become big-

ger, these are often replaced by conduits or pipes running the whole length of the structure, with offshoot pipes running into the lock to give an even discharge of water. Old locks may be manually operated but new ones are worked by hydraulic power.

Locks vary tremendously in size from about 126 by 17 feet (38 by 5 metres) on small canals to the giant locks on the Mississippi River in America, which are 1,200 by 110 feet (366 by 33·5 metres).

# WHY is there more sea than land on the earth's surface?

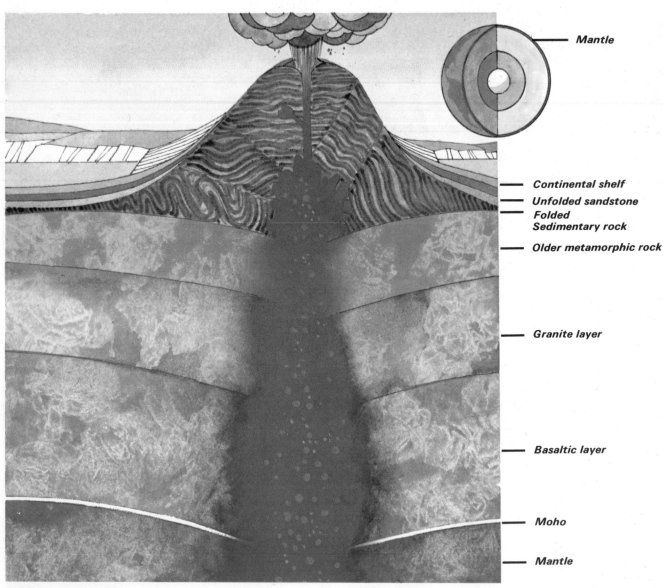

Mantle

Continental shelf
Unfolded sandstone
Folded Sedimentary rock
Older metamorphic rock

Granite layer

Basaltic layer

Moho

Mantle

## SEA AND LAND

The answer to this question lies in the composition of the rocks which make up the outer portion of the earth's crust. Over large areas of the earth's surface, these rocks are lightish in colour, relatively light in weight and are called granitic rocks, because granite is the most common type. Over still larger areas of the earth the rocks are darker, heavier and are called basaltic rocks, since among them basalt is the chief type.

We know that the earth at a depth of a few hundred miles below the surface is molten and that the surface or crustal rocks,

which are about 50 miles thick, are really floating on this liquid core.

The granitic rocks stand higher than the basaltic, just as a cork floats higher than wood, and therefore the granitic areas are the continents, and the basaltic, the ocean basins. If all crustal rocks were of the same composition, the earth's surface would be one vast ocean, more than a mile deep.

But why is there water in the sea? There are three reasons. First, molten rock holds much more water than when it hardens and cools. So, as the earth's crust

solidified, it gave off water vapour into the atmosphere. Secondly, the earth's gravity stops this vapour from escaping into space, just as it also retains the atmosphere we breathe. Thirdly, the pressure-temperature relationships on earth are such that the vapour is mainly in liquid form.

The water in the sea is salty because of the 2,000 million-years-old disintegration of the earth's crust. The soluble materials or salts remained in the ocean. The insoluble materials have formed sedimentary rocks and the ocean sediments.

# WHY does Venice have so many canals?
# WHY are there different kinds of soil?

## CANALS OF VENICE

Unlike most canals, those in Venice are not man-made. If anything, man has made the land round the canals.

In the 7th Century this North Italian town was no more than a series of tiny islands and mud flats. After the fall of the Roman Empire, political exiles sought refuge in the Venetian lagoons. Gradually a town emerged with many of its buildings having been constructed directly over the water, supported by massive foundations on the sea bed.

The canals between the groups of houses were left, and consequently, the only form of transport in Venice today is by boat.

The vibrations of motor vehicles would soon shatter the foundations of this beautiful city, which in some cases are precariously poised on nothing firmer than sand. In the days of the gondola all seemed well, but the wash produced by motor boats has greatly weakened Venice's structure.

To add to this historic city's problems, much of the main island is slowly sinking into the sea, largely because of the dredging and water pumping activities of a nearby industrial area.

The Italian government has now embarked on the difficult project of trying to keep this marvel of medieval and renaissance architecture and engineering afloat.

## DIFFERENT SOILS

The basic material of the surface of the earth is solid rock, and the surface of the landscape we see is nearly always the result of weathering, the action of sun, wind, frost, rain, ice or snow. Therefore, there are many kinds of soil depending upon the climate and the type of parent rock. There is also a third factor which influences the kind of soil formed. This is the vegetation.

The first step in weathering is the breaking down of the rock. Water plays an important part at this stage, either by freezing and shattering the rock as it expands or by washing away some of the minerals of which the rock is composed, thereby loosening its particles.

The climate is also important for most rocks contain much quartz as well as silicates. In a cold climate, the crystals of the silicates are dissolved more quickly than the quartz. In a hot moist climate however, the quartz is washed away and the silicates left behind. Every intermediate stage can be found between these two extreme types of soil.

Vegetation also plays its part by splitting rocks with its roots. Also dead branches and leaves fall on to the ground, decay and add a layer of humus to the soil, rich in nutrients which enable larger plants to grow. These larger plants support animals, some of which help to mix the soil still further.

There are other types of soil such as those formed from the silt deposited by rivers—alluvial soils— or where bogs and marshes occur. But one thing is common to all soils. They are very unstable if the vegetation which covers them and aids in their formation is removed. Then they are easily washed away and the result of centuries of slow development is lost.

# WHY does Holland have so many windmills?   WHY is a
## WHY could we sai

## WINDMILLS

The large number of windmills in Holland, or The Netherlands, is due to the fact that they were needed to pump water into the canals off the rich, low-lying land reclaimed from the sea. Windmills are still used for this purpose today, but pumps worked by electricity are more usual.

There is an old Dutch saying, "God made the world, but the Dutch made Holland". They certainly did make a great part of their land by dragging it from the sea, and the .battle to hold it never ceases. The name Netherlands (from the Dutch *nederland*) means low land, and more than one-third of Holland's land area of 12,530 square miles lies below sea level.

Along the coast are dunes of sand—nature's dykes—thrown up by normal tides. The Dutch plant them with marram grass, which holds the sand together with its long, strong, creeping roots. Behind the dunes the Dutch built three dykes of close-packed stone, clay and earth on wooden and concrete piles. The dyke nearest the sea is called a "waker". Behind it lies a "dreamer" and behind that again a "sleeper". Some of the dykes are 200–300 feet high and many have a road or, some, a railway running along the top.

In 1170 the North Sea swept into the country and formed the bay called the Zuyder Zee (South Sea). In 1421, another high tide flowed in to form the Hollandse Diep (Dutch Deep). The great spring tide of 1953 (two feet higher than any previously recorded) smashed the waker dykes, overflowed the dreamers and drowned about 1,900 people. About 50,000 were forced to flee from their homes.

A famous Dutch story tells of a brave boy who stood for hours with his hand thrust into a hole in a dyke and so prevented the sea from rushing in and widening the breach in the wall.

# mineral different from an animal?
# to the North Pole but not to the South Pole?

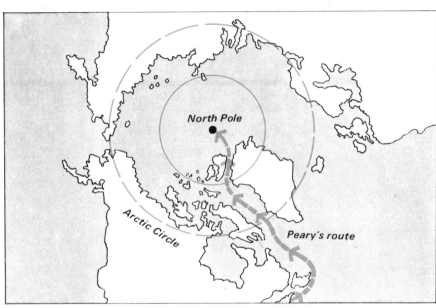

## THE POLES

A journey by sea to the North Pole with an ice-breaking ship of sufficient strength and large amounts of explosives is possible in theory, although it has never been achieved.

But the South Pole is in the middle of a great land mass, the continent of Antarctica. This uninhabited land surface varies from basins more than 8,000 feet below sea level to mountains well over 13,000 feet high.

The South Pole was first reached, after a 53-day march, by a Norwegian party led by Raold Amundsen, in December 1911. Amundsen's expedition travelled on foot and on sledges drawn by dogs. It beat Captain Robert Scott's party by a month.

An American party first reached the North Pole, but there is no absolute proof which one it was. The honour is most often given to the team led by Robert E. Peary who reached the Pole on April 6, 1909. Claims that Dr. F. A. Cook reached the spot with two Eskimos, two sledges and 26 dogs in April, 1908 are now generally doubted.

## ANIMAL AND MINERAL

A mineral is different from an animal in as much as it does not breathe and does not move. An animal is described as a living organism while a mineral is an inanimate organism.

Both minerals and animals can be classified exclusively in terms of their component chemicals. So in purely chemical terms a mineral cannot be described as dead because the atoms and molecules within are not dormant. They are capable of change and can even transform a mineral's shape.

But apart from chemical change the mineral, unlike the animal, cannot move.

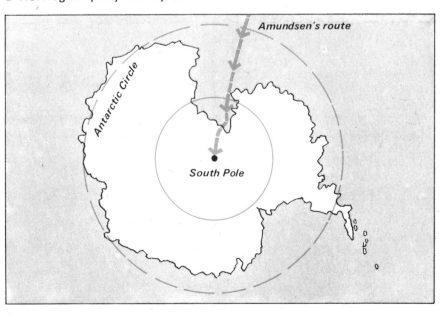

## AYER'S ROCK

The colour of Ayer's Rock alters continually according to the atmospheric conditions and the changing angle of the sun. The rock is an immense sandstone boulder rising 1,143 feet out of the flatness of the plain near the centre of Australia.

It is normally red, and measures over five miles round the base with relatively gentle slopes which can be easily scaled. The most dramatic effects occur at sunrise, when the sun's rays inflame the rock to a burning crimson, and at sunset, when marvellous purple shadows overlay the glowing blood-red monolith. The colours of the rock vary from a yellowish-ochre through all the various shades of oranges and reds to a deep purple and to black.

Ayer's rock is now one of Australia's most popular tourist attractions, though visitors of one kind or another have been travelling far for centuries to see the massive shape. There was a time when it was regarded with great awe as a religious shrine. People from the local tribes came to the caves around its base to worship and to decorate the walls with paintings. The rock was discovered by an Englishman, W. G. Gosse, in 1873 and named after Sir Henry Ayers, then Prime Minister of South Australia. The spot was so remote and inaccessible that for years few people ever visited the rock. Now they come by car and aeroplane and the rock forms part of the Ayer's Rock — Mount Olga National Park, 487 square miles in area, where the local plant and animal life is strictly protected.

Desert oak, mulga, mallee, bloodwood and spinifex are some of the exotic names of the plants that grow here. No less strange are the names and appearance of the animals—kangaroo, wallaby, bandicoot and euros.

*This great highway through Brazil will greatly disturb the ecological balance of the jungle.*

## have different shapes?    WHY do we study ecology?

6

### SHAPES OF CLOUDS

Clouds vary in shape according to their height and temperature, and they contain minute drops of water or ice particles or a combination of both. And, of course, their formation is greatly affected by wind changes.

There are basically three groups of clouds: high clouds between 17,000 and 45,000 feet (cirrus, cirro-cumulus and cirro-stratus); middle clouds between 7,000 and 23,000 feet (alto-cumulus, alto-stratus and nimbo-stratus); and low clouds up to 7,000 feet (strato-cumulus, stratus, cumulus and comulo-nimbus. Their height and temperature decide how much pressure is exerted on them by the atmosphere.

Finally, the shapes of clouds differ according to the time of day. Towards evening clouds tend to thin out, rise a little and flatten out.

### ECOLOGY

Ecology is concerned with the relationship between living things and their environment. This leads directly to the conservation of natural resources which is one of the most important problems facing the world today. Plants, animals and men are so closely associated and dependent upon each other that the ecologist's range of study is world-wide, although each special field has its own techniques.

The word ecology is derived from the Greek *oikos*, meaning house. Branches of ecology include types of environment, relationships between certain organisms and plants, game conservation, overcultivation, overpopulation and hundreds of others.

Most fields of study are inextricably bound up with the destiny of man. As it is such an enormous subject there is a danger that the information obtained will not be available soon enough to ensure proper conservation.

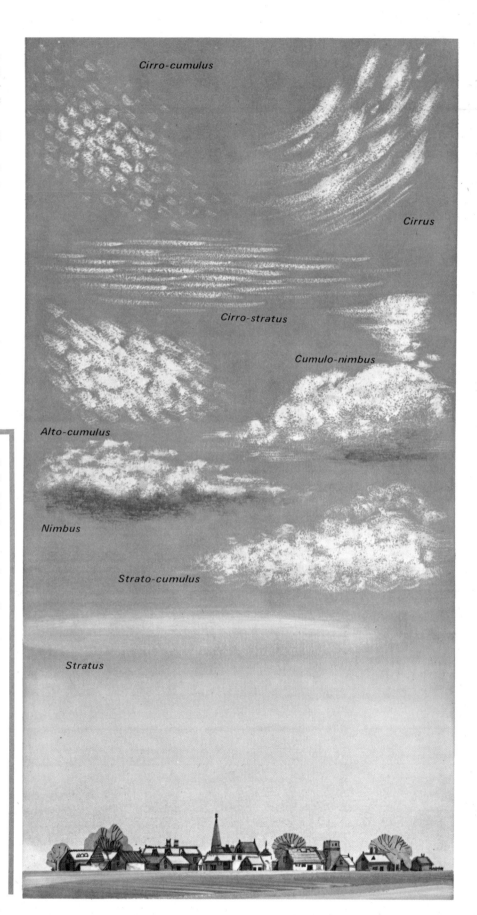

Cirro-cumulus

Cirrus

Cirro-stratus

Cumulo-nimbus

Alto-cumulus

Nimbus

Strato-cumulus

Stratus

# WHY were early maps decorated? WHY are some wells
## WHY does a compass point north–south?

## EARLY MAPS

Many early maps were decorated because the map-makers or cartographers had little real idea of geography and presented the world in symbolical terms. One map of Roman times showed the world as a T within an O. The O represented the ocean boundaries of the earth and the T the known world, with the Mediterranean as the upright and the horizontal bar as the meridian from the Nile to the River Don. Jerusalem was at the centre and elaborate decorations often included Paradise and the Last Judgment.

As the shapes of more coastlines were discovered, the unexplored land masses behind them were often filled in by map-makers with decorative portrayals of imagined animals and vegetation. The seas contained monsters and pictures of ships.

Even when maps became more accurate, decorations survived because cartographers saw their craft as a mixture of science and art.

Some maps were specially commissioned to be given as gifts to noble patrons or sovereigns. Unlike ordinary maps for use at sea, these special productions were magnificently decorated, with the seas and lands full of fabulous animals and the winds portrayed as human. The houses and ships shown were usually accurate pictures of those in use at the time the maps were made.

*An elaborately decorated map of the Middle East*

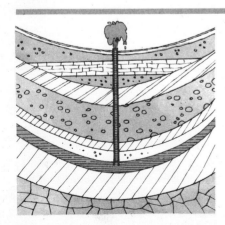

## ARTESIAN WELLS

Artesian wells are those from which water flows freely. These wells are man-made and are created by boring into the rock to a channel that is lower than the water source.

The resulting artesian well has the advantage over vertical wells of not requiring a pump. The water will pour out naturally without the aid of any mechanism until the well runs dry. For this reason artesian wells, although often several hundred feet deep, may be only a few inches wide. This prevents undue loss of water.

The term "artesian well" is derived from Artesium, the ancient name for Artois in Northern France, where a famous free-flowing well was excavated early in the 12th Century.

# alled artesian wells?
## WHY does India have monsoons?

## COMPASS

When the magnetic needle of a compass is allowed to move freely it will automatically place itself in line with the earth's magnetic field, one end pointing to the magnetic North Pole while the other indicates the South.

Natural magnets, such as loadstone or pieces of iron which have been touched by a loadstone, are to be found the world over. It was the discovery that loadstone would always place itself so as to lie in a magnetic north-to-south position that led to the invention of the magnet.

During the 15th Century it was realized that the magnetic North Pole and the Geographic North Pole were not exactly in the same place. The small angle between the two is known by seamen as "the variation". Some experts have claimed, however, that the Chinese were already aware of the existence of variation as early as the 11th Century. Again, in the 15th Century, it became apparent that the earth itself was a great magnet.

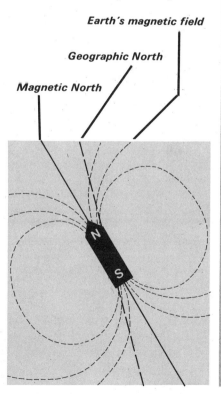

Earth's magnetic field

Geographic North

Magnetic North

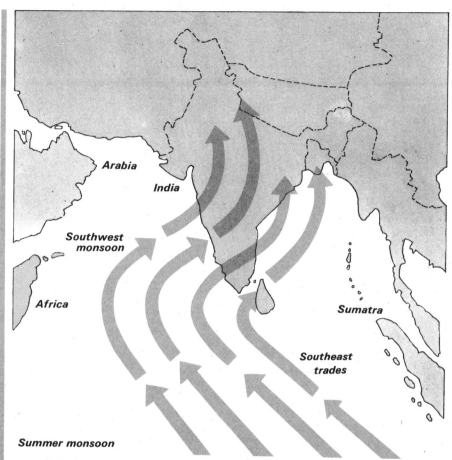

Arabia

India

Southwest monsoon

Africa

Sumatra

Southeast trades

Summer monsoon

## MONSOONS

The seasonal winds of south-west Asia known as monsoons are associated particularly with India because of the tremendous effects they have on the lives of the inhabitants. The winds are drawn to India by changes in the temperature of the great land mass. A good monsoon season with plenty of rain means a comparatively good supply of food. A bad monsoon with little rain means a bad rice crop and, perhaps, starvation for many millions.

Monsoon comes from the Arabic *mausim*, meaning season. The summer season monsoon is a great inrush of moisture-laden air from the ocean. The winter monsoon blows from the land to the sea.

In India there are three seasons: the hot dry season from March to June; the hot wet season from June to November; and the cool dry season from December to March. During the hot dry season the great plains of northern India become like a furnace and a region of low pressure develops.

By mid-June, the pressure is low all the way to the Equator and draws the south-east trade winds to India, filled with water-vapour as they cross the Indian Ocean. When they meet the hot dry air over India, violent thunderstorms result, followed by steady rain in July. By November India has received three-quarters of its annual rainfall.

Then the land mass cools and the high pressure attracts the north east trade winds. These bring no rain to India except to the Coromandel Coast and Ceylon, where the rainfall in late September is heavy, because the winds have picked up water vapour as they move across the wide expanse of the Bay of Bengal.

# WHY does the Mediterranean Sea look blue and the Atlant
## WHY are pebbles on a beach round? WH

## MEDITERRANEAN

The blueness of the Mediterranean and the greenness of the Atlantic Ocean are mainly due to the different amounts of sunlight reaching the water's surface.

Owing to their different geographic positions, the Mediterranean is far more often directly exposed to sunlight than the Atlantic. The blue colour of the sea is the result of the molecules of light scattering in the water.

The green colour of the Atlantic comes from decayed plants on the ocean bed. When these aquatic plants decompose, yellow pigments are released. It is this yellow, mixed with the already murky blue of the Atlantic that creates the characteristic green colour of that ocean.

## AGE OF FOSSILS

It is possible to estimate the relative age of fossils, that is whether they came before or after a particular period, because most fossils are found in sedimentary rocks. These are rocks made of sediment which has been compressed or cemented together in layers.

Older rock layers, or strata, are usually at the bottom. So each layer is younger than the layer below it and older than the one above. Fossils may be present in igneous rock (hardened volcanic lavas) and metamorphic rocks (formed by pressure and heat within the earth) but they are usually destroyed.

Telling the age of fossils in terms of years, or absolute time, is a much bigger problem. But scientists use several methods. The tree ring method, counting annual growth rings, can give a scientist a reasonably accurate date back to about 3,000 years ago.

The varve method, based on counting the annual layers of sand and clay deposited in a lake, bay

or river by melting glaciers, can be used for deposits less than about 15,000 years old. Similar calculations based on the rate of sedimentation, erosion, salt accumulation etc. have been successfully applied to very much older rocks.

The third method is concerned with radioactive decomposition

and is based on actual changes in some of the rock elements or in the fossils themselves. Radioactive uranium gradually changes to uranium lead, radiocarbon to nitrogen and so on. From the proportion of uranium lead to uranium in the rock we can date the oldest rocks and fossils, nearly 3,000 million years old.

cean look green ?   **WHY** is it possible to estimate
vould you go to Death Valley ?          the age of fossils ?

## PEBBLES

The pebbles that are to be found on a beach are invariably round and smooth owing to the constant battering they have received from the sea.

Originally pebbles were part of much larger rocks, but various natural phenomena, such as earthquakes and volcanoes, have gradually broken them down. Caught in the movement of the sea, and constantly rubbed against other hard materials, the pebbles finally lose their irregularities and present a smooth round surface.

Many of the rocks of today will be pebbles in thousands of years' time, and many of today's pebbles will eventually be turned into sand by the constant, wearing action of the sea.

## DEATH VALLEY

You would go to Death Valley, as do half a million visitors each year, to look at its magnificently varied scenery and to recapture the flavour of those days of privation and hardship which gave the valley its name.

Death Valley National Monument is in the state of California in the U.S.A. In its 3,000 square miles can be found sheer-walled canyons, desert springs and sands, an extinct volcano, snow-topped mountain ranges, desolate wastes of salt crystals and gardens of fragile wild flowers.

There is a 200 square mile salt pan that contains the Western Hemisphere's lowest point—282 feet below sea level—and is the driest spot in the U.S.A.

Death Valley also contains long-abandoned mines, silent witnesses to the gold seekers of 1849 who lived and died in its inhospitable terrain. Coffin Canyon, Deadman Pass, Hells Gate, Starvation Canyon and Suicide Pass are names which perpetuate the despair and suffering of these pioneers.

66

# WHY did the continents drift apart? WHY is a seismograp

*Upper Carboniferous period*

*Eocene period*

*Lower Quaternary period*

## CONTINENTAL DRIFT

One of the most convincing explanations of why the continents drifted apart is that the earth expanded considerably after its creation. This theory can be illustrated by imagining the earth as a balloon and the continents as pieces of paper stuck on the outside. As the balloon is blown up the pieces of paper will grow farther apart.

Other theories suggest that the continents only appeared to drift apart because masses of land were drowned under volcanic waters. But it has been demonstrated that land masses are, in fact, made to drift, by the heat generated from the earth's interior and from earthquakes.

Probably a combination of various theories may be necessary to provide a complete explanation.

## SEISMOGRAPH

A seismograph is used to measure the vibrations of the earth and to locate the source of earth vibrations. Phenomena capable of being detected by a seismograph include earthquakes, volcanic eruptions, explosions such as bombs, powerful winds, violent storms at sea and even, in urban areas, traffic.

Thanks to the seismograph whole populations can be warned and prepared for a variety of natural disasters. Seismic observatories around the world, have provided information increasing our knowledge of the earth's structure.

The seismograph operates on one of two basically simple mechanisms which are devices responsive to strain and pendulums. The earliest form of seismograph known was developed in China in the 2nd Century.

There are many examples of the usefulness of seismographs in a wide variety of fields. They have been used to measure the thickness of the ice sheets covering the polar regions of the earth and, when used in conjunction with artificial explosions created under special test conditions, seismographs can help geologists trace oil fields.

## AVALANCHES

An avalanche occurs when a mass of snow which has built up on a mountain side begins to slip and finally to fall. There can also be avalanches of earth, stones, rock and ice, but usually the word is used to describe a rapid fall of snow.

Snow builds up to great thickness on steep slopes, especially if the surface is not smooth. Even a very small disturbance may set it in motion. The vibration of a passing vehicle, the movement of a man or animal, the fall of a tree branch or even a sound can cause thousands of tons of snow to crash down a mountainside.

The speed of an avalanche varies enormously, but some have been estimated to move at about 200 miles an hour. A big avalanche hurtles down the side of the mountain with a thunderous roar, crushing or sweeping away anything in its path.

The swiftly moving mass of snow pushes the air in front of it with such violence that it fans out sideways as well as driving directly ahead. This wind sometimes reaches a force almost equal to that of a tornado. This great wind is often a more powerful force of destruction than the avalanche itself.

seful? **WHY** do avalanches occur?
**WHY** do earthquakes only occur in certain places?

## EARTHQUAKES

Earthquakes occur mainly in the regions of the earth where mountains are being formed, and where the earth's crust is under strain.

Some mountains are formed of great thicknesses of folded sedimentary rock laid down beneath the sea. Heat currents deep within the earth are thought to suck down sections of the undersea crust and so produce great trenches thousands of feet deep. When the heat currents die away the material forming the bottom of the trench begins to rise because it is lighter in weight. Eventually it is thrust up as a mountain range.

This is never a smooth process

but is accompanied by great friction and heat, as well as by rending and shearing and tearing. The tearing and shearing of deep underground rocks connected with mountain formation cause earthquakes. Even small underground movements may produce violent surface shocks. The great Tokyo earthquake of 1923 which is believed to have killed 25 million people was caused by the twisting of a section of the earth's crust in Sagami Bay.

As might be expected, ocean trenches are the seat of a great many earthquakes, for there the earth's crust is in an unstable state.

Indeed all the deep earthquakes—those taking place more than 160 miles below the surface—originate around the Pacific trenches. About 90 per cent of the intermediate earthquakes (30 to 160 miles deep) also originate there, as do 40 per cent of the shallow earthquakes (less than 30 miles deep).

Some shallow and intermediate earthquakes are caused by volcanoes or by a slight shifting of layers of rock at a weak place or "fault" on the earth's surface. One of the most famous and widely publicized of these is the San Andreas fault on which San Francisco is built.

# Medicine and the Body

## KIDNEYS

Our kidneys perform four functions, of which the most obvious is the ejection of waste materials containing nitrogen from the body. They also keep the acid-base balance of the blood constant, and regulate the volume of circulating blood and the fluid content of the body as a whole. Finally they regulate pressure relationships between the blood and the tissues.

The kidneys, bean-shaped and about four inches long, lie on the back wall of the abdomen just above the waist, one on each side of the spinal column.

Blood enters the kidney by the renal artery. Some of its plasma is filtered off and, after other processes, ends as urine. The rest leaves the kidney by the renal vein to return to the heart. The urine collects in the central cavity (pelvis) of the kidney, passes down to the bladder via a tube (ureter) and is finally expelled.

A human being can survive without kidneys for only two or three weeks. Nearly one-fifth of the blood pumped out of the heart goes through the kidneys. The kidneys thus regulate the body fluid—a fluid which Claude Bernard (1813–1878), the great French physiologist, called our "internal environment".

## BRUISES

We bruise because the body has received a heavy blow which injures the bodily tissues without rupturing or tearing the outer covering of skin.

A bruise is a wound, and a wound may be defined as a breach in the continuity of any body tissue. Often the skin is cut or torn. But closed wounds, such as the rupturing of internal organs, may leave no visible external sign.

A bruise, or contusion of the skin, is caused by the rupture of the blood vessels in the deeper layers of the tissues under the skin. The blood escapes from the damaged vessels into the surrounding tissues and brings about discoloration of the skin, which at first goes red, and then "black and blue". As the blood pigments break down, the bruise changes to yellow and green, and eventually fades away. Usually bruises show in the area where the blow has fallen. But there are times when the blood will track along muscles and the planes of connective tissue, causing the bruise to appear some way away from the injury.

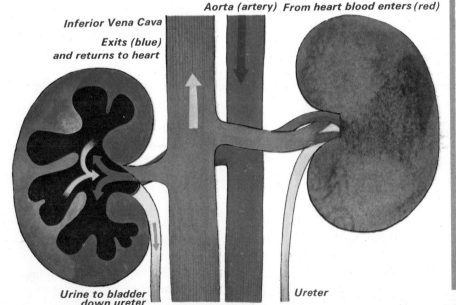

Aorta (artery) From heart blood enters (red)

Inferior Vena Cava
Exits (blue) and returns to heart

Urine to bladder down ureter

Ureter

# he knee or ankle swell up if injured?
## WHY do medicines come in different forms?

## KNEES AND ANKLES

The swelling of an injured joint, like a knee or an ankle, is caused by the multiplication of normal cells to cushion the affected part. This sudden increase is called hyperplasia. There is also a certain amount of internal bleeding as a result of the injury.

Swellings are divided into two main groups, false tumours and true tumours. The inflammatory swellings that appear after joint injuries belong to the first group, which includes bruises, black eyes, sprains, fractures and infectious swellings such as boils and abscesses. Swollen joints can be eased by the application of cold compresses, or pads, and ice packs. Firm bandages are used to give support.

True tumours or swellings are composed of masses of tissue developed from body cells which already exist. They have a tendency to keep growing. Some of these tumours have normal cells and are said to be benign or harmless. In others the cells are slightly different from their parents and the tumours are generally malignant.

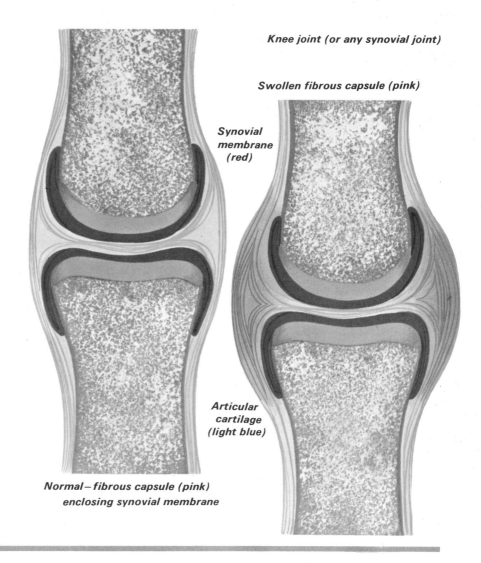

*Knee joint (or any synovial joint)*

*Swollen fibrous capsule (pink)*

*Synovial membrane (red)*

*Articular cartilage (light blue)*

*Normal — fibrous capsule (pink) enclosing synovial membrane*

## MEDICINAL FORMS

Medicine is given in different forms because of the necessity for convenience or for speed. It can be given by mouth (orally) in the form of tablets, capsules or draughts. It can be inhaled in the form of gases, fine aerosols or, very rarely, exceedingly fine powder. Injections of medicine are given subcutaneously (beneath the skin), intramuscularly or intravenously. Sometimes solid implants in the form of tablets may be placed subcutaneously. Injections may also be given in the spine or brain. Medicines can be given through the rectum as solids (suppositories) or enemas, or through the vagina as pessaries or douches. Finally, there are solutions, powders, creams and ointments which are placed locally on the skin.

Convenient medicines are those which can be taken or administered easily by the patient himself. Oral medicine and inhalations are convenient and a great deal of research is carried out to make these more palatable.

Manufacturers prefer oral preparations because they can be attractively coloured and flavoured and made impressively mysterious in size and shape. They can also be code-stamped or named for identification. Injections have to be sterile and kept in appropriate containers and are therefore relatively expensive.

# WHY do some people go bald? WHY do we usually get WHY should you not watch television in a darkened room?

*A gathering of the Bald-Headed Men's Society at the French town of Villechauve.*

## BALD PEOPLE

There are two reasons why people may go bald. The live hair germ centres have either been permanently destroyed or they have been temporarily damaged.

Permanent baldness or alopecia occurs in more than 40 per cent of men and may affect the whole head. In women it affects the crown of the head only and never leads to complete loss of hair. Three factors often lead to permanent baldness—heredity, age and hormone balance. There is no cure. Other causes of permanent baldness may be injuries or diseases which produce severe scarring, inborn lack of hair development and severe injuries to the hair germ centres by chemicals.

Temporary hair loss often occurs after a high fever, thyroid disease or tuberculosis, but it grows again in most cases after the disease is cured.

Drugs, X-rays, malnutrition and some skin diseases can also cause temporary hair loss, but usually it grows again within a year.

There is also a disease called alopecia areata, in which the hair falls out in patches all over the head. Usually the germ centres have been injured only temporarily, and in 99 per cent of cases the hair grows again without treatment.

Baldness may occur at almost any time of life after childhood.

## MEASLES

We usually get measles or chickenpox only once because our bodies manufacture special chemical defences called antibodies. These antibodies are selective and are effective only against the particular microbe they have been formulated to fight. After the battle is won, the antibodies remain in the bloodstream, ready to repel another attack.

The antibodies are large complex protein molecules. One group, the antitoxins, act as antidotes, neutralizing the poisons that the microbes release into the body. The other group, the agglutinins, clump the microbes together so that they fall easy prey to the white

# measles or chicken-pox only once?
## WHY do we produce saliva?

## TELEVISION

You should not watch television in a darkened room because you will not see the picture so clearly. The human eye functions best, and is able to see detail most acutely when viewing white light. So a lightish background makes for a better picture.

Of course, it is unwise to have the source of light shining directly on to the television set because some of the rays will be reflected and spoil the picture.

Viewing in a dark room can also cause an unpleasant glare. The intense light coming from a television screen against a black background causes a certain amount of stray light to be reflected internally from structures within the eye on to the retina. (The retina is the delicate tissue containing the photo receptors.) The effect is similar, if less intense, to that produced by a car with undipped headlights.

A third disadvantage of a darkened background is that "flicker" on the television screen becomes more apparent and can cause severe eye fatigue. In certain quite rare cases this "flicker" effect can produce epileptic fits.

blood cells, or leukocytes. These leukocytes develop in the bone marrow and are always present in the blood.

Some of them surround the infected area and quarantine it by making a wall with their own bodies. Within the barricade, the rest of them attack the microbes and eat them up. Like tiny amoebas, they crawl about and stretch out foot-like projections called pseudopods which they use to engulf bacteria and digest them. This explains their other name phagocyte, or eating cell. Each phagocyte can eat about a dozen bacteria this way—a process called phagocytosis.

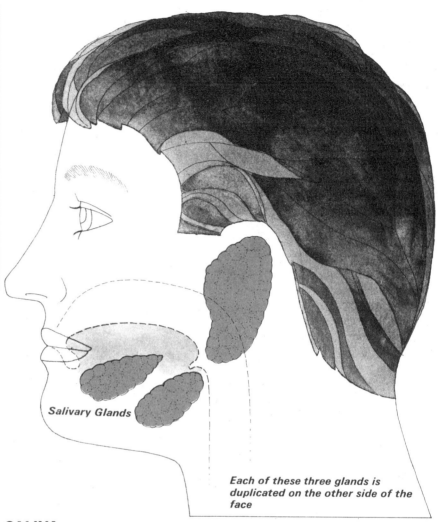

*Salivary Glands*

**Each of these three glands is duplicated on the other side of the face**

## SALIVA

Saliva, the watery secretion produced in our mouths, has many functions. It moistens the mouth and tongue, making sure that the mucous membrane does not dry or crack. It also moistens our food so that it can be moulded into an egg-shaped mass (or bolus) for swallowing, and it lubricates the bolus so that it can be swallowed easily.

By means of the enzyme ptyalin, which it contains, saliva begins the digestion of carbohydrates inside the food. Saliva also acts as a solvent to make tasting food easier, for the taste buds are stimulated only by dissolved substances.

It is a cleansing agent, washing away particles inside the mouth. If salivation is stopped, for instance in the case of a high fever, the mouth becomes dirty and tastes and smells foul. If salivation slows down, our mouths feel dry, and we know we need water.

Saliva is secreted in the three pairs of salivary glands. The largest of these are the irregularly shaped parotid glands which are packed tightly into a space between the ear and the top of the jawbone. The glands are encased in an inelastic covering and that is why they are extremely painful if they swell. The next pair are the submandibular glands which are egg-shaped and lie under the front of the jawbone, and the third pair, the almond-shaped sublingual glands, lie on the floor of the mouth between the tongue and the jawbone.

# WHY aren't people the same colour? WHY do we turn whit

## COLOUR OF PEOPLE

People vary in the colour of their skin because of a network of pigment-forming cells called melanocytes. This network is interspersed between, and lies underneath, the cells of the deepest layer of the epidermis, or outer skin, which is called the stratum basale.

The melanocytes have slender, branchlike extensions which touch one another and also extend upwards between the cells of the deeper portions of the epidermis. There are about 1,000 to 3,000 melanocytes in each square millimetre of skin, and each one produces the dark pigment melanin formed as a result of oxidation.

This oxidation is catalysed by a copper-containing enzyme called tyrosinase, which gives the reddish spectrum of colour changes. Various stages of formation produce is pale yellow, tawny, orange, reddish, brown and, finally, intensely black.

Human skin contains greater or lesser amounts of melanin. In fair-skinned races the deep skin layer of melanocytes contains very little pigment. In the darker races, the deposits are heavy, and other melanocytes are to be found in the upper layers of the epidermis.

# when frightened? WHY do we get indigestion?

Melanin is a natural protection from harmful sunrays and, on exposure to sunlight, man's skin normally undergoes gradual tanning. This increase of melanin pigment, helps to safeguard underlying tissues. In blondes and redheads the pigment cells respond only slightly and rather unevenly. The consequence of this may be a "freckling" effect rather than a sun-tanned look.

## WHITE WITH FEAR

We turn white when we are frightened because the blood in our cheeks is diverted to do a more urgent job. At the same time our hearts begin to beat much faster, and we breathe more quickly.

When we sit still, our hearts beat at about 70 or 80 times a minute, pumping the blood through our bodies. The blood carries nourishment from food, and oxygen from the air we breathe, both of which are vitally necessary for the body to function.

If we take violent exercise, our muscles need to work much harder and faster than when we are sitting or walking. They therefore need extra nourishment and oxygen. The nerves carry the message to that part of the brain called the hypothalamus, the centre of an automatic nervous system in control of internal bodily functions such as the pumping of the heart, breathing and digestion.

Impulses from the hypothalamus travel down the spinal cord and excite other nerve cells—"sympathetic" neurons—which end in the centre or medulla of the adrenal glands just above the kidneys. These glands release the hormone adrenalin into the bloodstream which causes the heart to beat faster and more efficiently, dilates air passages in the lungs and the blood vessels that supply the muscles, and increases the concentration of energy-giving glucose in the blood.

In fact, when we are frightened, exactly the same physical changes take place and our bodies are immediately and efficiently prepared for the violent exercise of flight or fight without any voluntary effort on our part.

## INDIGESTION

Indigestion is most often brought about by interference with a marvellous piece of engineering contained in 30 to 32 feet of continuous hollow tubing called the alimentary canal.

In this system the food is broken down, churned, diluted, dissolved and chemically split into simpler compounds which can be absorbed into the blood.

The alimentary canal is formed of membrane which has to resist a chemistry that dissolves bone, gristle, animal and vegetable matter far tougher than the membrane itself. The stomach's gastric juice, one of the chief agents in digestion, has a high concentration of hydrochloric acid. This can dissolve a hard-boiled egg in a few minutes.

Why does it not dissolve the stomach? One reason seems to be that the stomach secretes not only acid but also ammonia, an equally powerful alkali which acts as a neutralizing agent.

This powerful gastric juice can be hindered by many causes, with the result that we may get the pains we know as indigestion.

The alimentary canal makes its preparations for a meal well in advance. The sight and smell and even the thought of food set the salivary and gastric juices flowing, while the stomach blushes in anticipation as the glands begin working and the capillaries widen to bring in an extra blood supply for the activity of digestion.

But the prospect of an unappetizing meal or disagreeable company, and the emotions of worry, irritation, anger and fear may stop these preparations. They may even cause the stomach to turn pale. Indigestion is the result.

We may also get indigestion if we eat too quickly without chewing our food or eat too many foods which are difficult to digest, thus overloading and disrupting the system.

# WHY do animals need oxygen?  WHY is it harder to walk
# WHY can you not breathe when you swallow?

## OXYGEN

We must have oxygen to live. Every living animal cell needs oxygen for its vital metabolic activities (the process of converting fuel to energy), and every cell must also get rid of its carbon dioxide, the gaseous waste of its metabolism.

In the simple animal forms each cell gets oxygen for itself out of the surrounding environment and gives off carbon dioxide in the same way.

In the more highly developed organisms a special mechanism makes the exchange of oxygen and carbon dioxide on behalf of the entire body, and a carrier fetches the oxygen and carries away the waste for all the cells. The carrier is the blood in its circulatory system, and the special exchange mechanism is the respiratory system with the lungs as the key organs.

We have developed from water-dwelling creatures and still spend the first nine months from our conception lying in a bath of warm fluid, called the amnion, receiving the oxygen necessary for the cells to do their work from our mothers.

In fact, we are still essentially water-dwellers, carrying our watery environment around within us, inside our skins. Because we have evolved lungs instead of gills we are able to live on land, but the air must be sufficiently rich in oxygen—about 97 per cent. Above 8,000 feet breathing begins to become difficult and the symptoms of mountain sickness, headache, nausea and vomiting may appear.

If we did nothing but rest, needing only a minimum supply of air, we would still need 300 quarts of oxygen every day. In a single minute of ordinary activity half a pint of oxygen has to be transferred from the air to the blood. For this half pint the lungs must process about five quarts of air every minute. An athlete running a race at sea level breathes as much as 120 quarts of air a minute to get the oxygen he needs to keep him going, which shows the importance of healthy lungs.

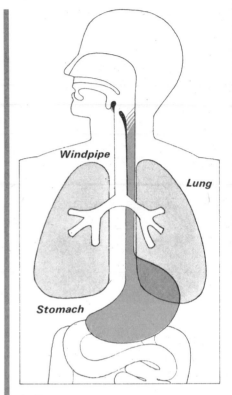

Windpipe

Lung

Stomach

## BREATHING

You are not able to breathe when you swallow because your respiratory (breathing) system is closely linked to your alimentary (nourishing) system. In fact, both the air you breathe and the food you eat travel down the pharynx, a wide muscular tube situated behind the nose and mouth.

The air must reach the larynx or "voice box" on its way to the trachea (principal air passage) and the lungs, while the food has to go by way of the oesophagus (gullet) and stomach. Obviously, some kind of device must be used to prevent the two from becoming mixed up.

Swallowing temporarily interrupts breathing by closing the air passages while food is propelled from the mouth to the gullet and stomach. If a particle of food goes the wrong way the lungs respond immediately by trying to expel the food with a cough. Also some air does find its way to the stomach and can, if excessive, cause flatulence or "wind".

## UP AND DOWNHILL

It is harder to walk uphill than downhill because you must lift the weight of your body and to do this requires greater energy than that needed for walking on the level. To create this greater energy your muscles require to give extra lift, your heart has more work to do to feed the blood cells and remove their waste matter and your lungs have more work to do to remove the carbon dioxide from your heart and replenish it with oxygen. That is why the steeper the climb and the more concentrated the effort, the more quickly you breathe. If you are out of condition you start to "pant" to gulp in extra oxygen. In comparison to the energy necessary for walking on a horizontal plane, the total value of the extra energy needed for climbing is the weight of your body times the height you are to reach.

The steeper the incline of the hill, the quicker you use this extra energy. It is therefore harder for you to walk up a steep hill than a gentle one, although the energy used up in either case, where the height to be reached is the same, is identical.

When you walk downhill, very little energy is needed because the weight of your body carries you down the slope. Of course, this is the pull of gravity that is helping you down, in the same way that you have to overcome the force of gravity when you walk up a steep hill.

uphill than downhill? WHY do we have loops and whorls? WHY is it said "an apple a day keeps the doctor away"?

## LOOPS AND WHORLS

The skin's surface is marked by a series of fine lines and ridges which deepen with age. The pattern on the tips of the fingers is peculiar to each individual and is used as a means of identification. In fact, the ridges of the skin on the lower finger joints and the toe prints are also unique, as are palm prints and foot prints. But fingerprints are by far the most simple and effective identification method.

Each ridge of the outer skin (epidermis) is dotted with sweat pores and anchored to the inner skin (dermis) by a double row of peglike objects called papillae. Injuries which affect the epidermis do not alter the ridge structure, and the original pattern returns in the new skin. If the papillae are destroyed, however, the ridges will disappear.

There are five general pattern shapes or types: the arch, the tented arch, the radial loop, the ulnar loop and the whorl. Whorls are usually circular or spiral, arches are shaped like a mound or hill and tented arches have a spike or "steeple" in the centre. Loops have concentric hairpin-shaped ridges and are divided into "radial" and "ulnar" to denote their slopes in relation to the radius and ulna bones of the forearm. Ulnar loops slope towards the little finger side of the hand and radial loops slope towards the thumb.

The pattern on our fingertips

*Arches*

*Loops*

*Whorls*

*Composites*

remains the same from birth until death, barring deliberate or accidental destruction of the papillae. Fingerprints therefore provide a positive identification, and the practice of fingerprinting (dactyloscopy) is an essential part of police procedure.

## AN APPLE A DAY

The old rhyme, "An apple a day keeps the doctor away", was a polite way of saying that this would help to prevent constipation since it was believed that the juice of a raw apple aided the fermentation of undigested foods.

Although we might query such a sweeping statement these days, apples *are* good for you, but it is the dentist more than the doctor they keep away! Dentists will tell you that biting on a crisp crumbly apple is an effective method of removing food particles from between the teeth. Eating an apple after meals and cleaning your teeth night and morning is the best protection you can give them. To say this is not to deny the overall value of an apple and the presence of Vitamin C (ascorbic acid), as well as other minerals, lends some weight to the old adage. Some say you feel well in direct proportion to the amount of Vitamin C in your tissues.

# WHY are some people colour blind? WHY do we sometime

## COLOUR BLINDNESS

Scientists think that some people are colour blind because they have an abnormality of the three pigments in the cones in the retina of the eye which, it is supposed, are necessary for colour vision.

The theory of colour vision depends on the fact that any colour in the spectrum can be matched by a mixture of three pure spectral colours of variable intensity but fixed wavelength. In colour blind persons, all three pigments are present, but are of an intensity different from normal.

They can see all the colours, but have difficulty in distinguishing between red, green and yellow, or between blue, green and yellow. Absence of one or more pigments is rare but does exist, while the complete absence of colour vision resulting from lack of cones in the retina sometimes occurs.

Most colour blind people are ignorant of their abnormality until it is demonstrated to them by means of a special test. Usually it is not a great handicap. But there are situations, and jobs, such as an air pilot, in which it may be important to distinguish colours quickly.

*This chart is used for detecting red-green colour deficiency. People with normal colour vision will see a mug and a tea pot. Those affected will see only a mug. It should be noted this is only one of a series of tests for testing colour vision and is not sufficient by itself to prove defective colour vision.*

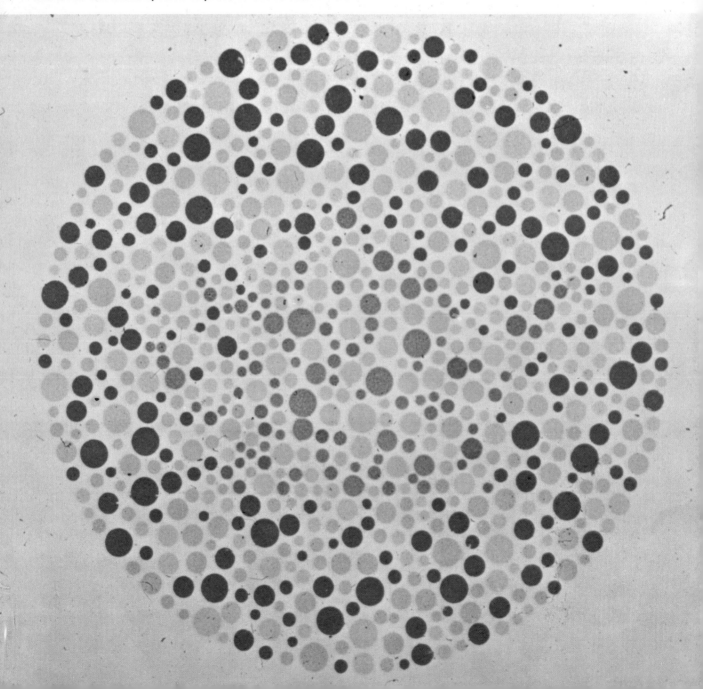

## SCRATCHING

One of the commonest causes of an itchy skin is an allergy. The word was coined in 1906 by Professor Clemens von Puquet of Vienna to describe a special state of exceptional sensitivity of the body to certain substances brought into contact with it. Such substances are called allergens, and include furs, feathers, foods, dust, pollens and drugs.

Most people have experienced allergy in some degree at some time, and about 10 per cent of the population show more or less permanent symptoms of allergic illnesses.

An allergic reaction is always the same, no matter what has caused it. The reason is thought to be that a process similar to the antibody reaction is set off, not in the bloodstream but on the surface of the body cells.

This allergen-antibody damages the cell walls and sets free a substance called histamine which produces two responses. It allows fluid to escape from the blood vessels into the surrounding tissues and it brings about an involuntary contraction or spasm of certain muscles.

When contact with an allergen is external we develop an itch which may be caused by light, heat, cold, hair or fur. It can also be caused by eating foods such as shellfish, mushrooms and strawberries or by an allergy to some drugs and medicines. If the allergen is inhaled there may be, as in hay fever, an excessive secretion of mucous, or, as in asthma, a severe spasm of the lung's air passages.

A true allergen is always a protein, a complex substance which forms an essential part of animal and plant tissues, but the abnormal reaction is produced only by a particular substance or group of substances.

## SMILING

We smile to show our pleasure or amusement in something or with someone. In fact, smiling seems to be an expression with which we are born, for most babies smile during the first weeks of life.

Charles Darwin (1809–1882), the great English naturalist who established the theory of organic evolution in his work, *Origin of Species*, also published, in 1872, a book, *Expression of the Emotions in Man and Animals*, in which he studied the facial expressions of men and animals. Most of the experiments connected with facial expression have been based on this book.

It has been suggested that a baby begins to realize within its first year of life that a smile is a "good" expression because it is greeted with pleasure by mother or nurse. The smile develops, some time after the twentieth week of life, into laughter but there are great differences between the frequency of laughter and smiles in individuals.

As the child grows up, the action of smiling becomes bound up with a growing awareness of what is socially acceptable in certain situations. In an adult it is often difficult to be certain whether the response is truly emotional or not. Recently different kinds of smiles have been more closely observed. It is notable that the pattern of the smile alters, according to the situation, from a wide spontaneous grin akin to laughter to a tight, nervous grimace which is nearer to a reaction of fear.

# WHY do we grow old? WHY are young babies fed on milk

*This is a detail from Dürer's picture of his ageing mother.*

## BABIES AND MILK

Young babies are fed on milk because it is their natural food. The females of all backboned animals whose young are nourished with milk, store this fluid in their breasts, or mammae. The milk of each species of mammal is a complete food for its own young after birth.

Although the same ingredients are present in the milk of all mammals, the proportions differ a great deal. The ingredients are water, protein, fat and milk sugar. Milk protein contains all the essential amino-acids. The fat globules remain enclosed in a soft curd which milk forms in the stomachs of the young, so that digestion can proceed smoothly without the disturbance that fatty foods often cause.

Human babies, if not fed by their mothers, may be fed with pasteurized cow's milk, diluted and sweetened, or a liquid reconstituted from laboratory-prepared dried milk. In various countries babies have been fed on milk from the ass, goat, water-buffalo, reindeer, caribou, sheep, camel, llama, bitch and mare.

Other foods have been tried. In the 17th Century babies were fed on pap (bread cooked in water) or, as a French doctor advised, bread cooked in beer! After about four or five months human babies are gradually weaned from an exclusive diet of milk and given other forms of nourishment.

## GROWING OLD

Scientists have evolved three main theories to explain why we grow old. The first concerns the loss of cells or of irreplaceable parts. Brain cells undoubtedly die off in their hundreds of thousands and cannot be manufactured again after a very infantile stage in human life.

However, this cannot be the complete explanation because people who suffer heavy damage to brain and body do not necessarily show the effects of ageing. Moreover, animals have totally different ageing rates, but suffer cell destruction at similar speeds.

A second theory concerns mutations or alterations. A dividing cell does not always divide correctly. All kinds of errors may creep in, aided by natural radiation. Sometimes the mutated cells may be harmful or put out of commission, with powerful effects on other cells, such as the endocrine glands or constituents of the blood. In the 1960s this theory was supported by the discovery that 10 per cent of the cells of very old women had lost an X chromosome.

A third explanation, which is not now so widely believed, is concerned with the accumulation of unwanted chemicals. It is suggested that some vital substances can only be replaced at cell division and that a general decline in the rate of cell division could lead either to a lack of needed substances or an excess of unwanted ones.

# WHY do we vaccinate against smallpox?

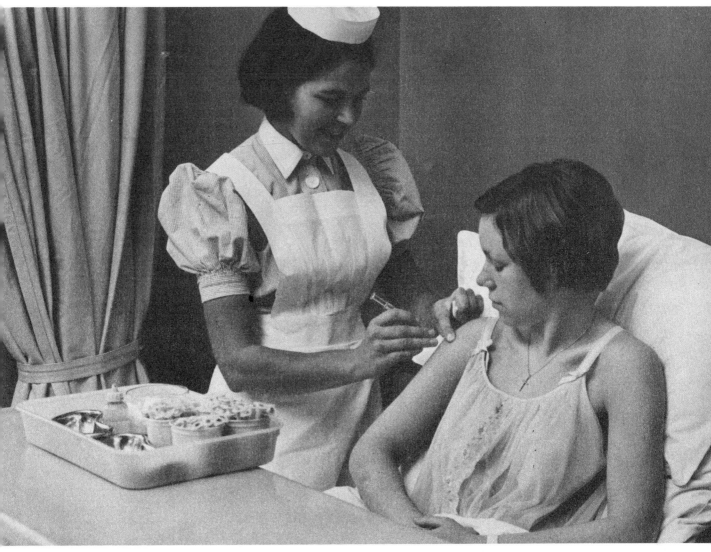

## VACCINATION

We vaccinate against smallpox to allow the body to develop antibodies which will make it more or less immune to attack from the disease. In fact, by vaccination or inoculation we mean that a person is injected with the organism that causes the disease or its toxin (poison). This organism is modified physically or chemically, so that, without doing any damage, it triggers the body's immunizing defences. We call these modified cultures vaccines.

Vaccination against smallpox was first carried out in the East. Poisonous material taken from the blisters of a mild case of smallpox was inserted into the arm of the person to be protected. This produced a mild case of smallpox and enabled the body to manufacture the antibodies.

Vaccination was introduced into England in 1721 by Lady Mary Wortley Montagu, wife of the British ambassador to Turkey, who had her own children inoculated at Constantinople. However, this method could result in a severe or fatal attack of the disease.

Dr. Edward Jenner took the next step in 1796 when he inoculated a boy named James Phipps with poisonous matter from the arm of Sarah Nelmes, a dairymaid suffering from cowpox (a mild disease closely allied to smallpox).

Some weeks later he inoculated James Phipps with smallpox, but the boy did not contract the disease.

In 1798 Jenner published a book on his experiments, and the practice of vaccination spread throughout the world. The principle has been applied to many diseases. Babies and young children are particularly susceptible to complications from whooping cough and diphtheria, so they are immunized soon after birth. Poliomyelitis (infantile paralysis), cholera, yellow fever, and typhoid are all dangerous diseases which inoculation has been able to control.

80

# WHY do we become sea-sick?     WHY do we have wax ir

## SEA-SICKNESS

We become sea-sick because our balancing organs, the labyrinthine portions of the inner ear, are disturbed by out-of-level movements, by sudden turning movements, and by sudden changes in movements in a straight line, either horizontal or vertical.

The three semicircular canals, filled with fluid, are set on different planes in the ear. When sudden movements occur, each canal is affected differently. The nerve endings have no time to convey information to the brain so giddiness is likely to occur.

Nowadays, seasickness comes under the general heading of motion sickness, a name invented by Sir Frederick Banting in 1939, which includes the discomfort people feel while travelling in all kinds of vehicles.

Sea-sickness may vary with individuals from slight uneasiness to complete prostration. The symptoms are pallor, cold sweating, nausea and vomiting. People who have lost their ear labyrinths because of disease do not become seasick. Others become resistant to it. We say they develop their "sea-legs", but it would appear to be an adjustment of the central nervous system rather than the organs of balance. Some people find it helpful to keep their gaze firmly fixed on a steady object.

*The red area in the diagram illustrates the semicircular canal, which is the major part of the inner ear. Its function is to help a person keep their balance through a delicate system of nerves. The sensation of sickness occurs when a conflict arises between the messages received by the brain through the nerves. The canals can just be seen on the right of the diagram below.*

## EAR WAX

Wax is deposited in our ear by special glands to prevent dust and similar foreign material from entering.

The part of the ear that we can see as a projecting flap on the side of the head is called the auricle. Leading from it is a short tunnel, the external auditory meatus or earhole, which is closed at its inner end by a thin membrane called the ear-drum, separating it from the inner ear.

This tunnel is lined with skin which, especially in men, carries hair and sebaceous glands, that is glands which produce an oily substance called sebum. The skin also contains specialized sweat glands (ceruminous glands), which secrete the brownish yellow wax.

Sometimes the glands secrete too much wax, and then it may collect in the external auditory meatus and deaden the hearing. As the ear is such a delicate instrument, the excess wax should be removed with a syringe by a doctor, although it can sometimes be softened by the application of warmed oil.

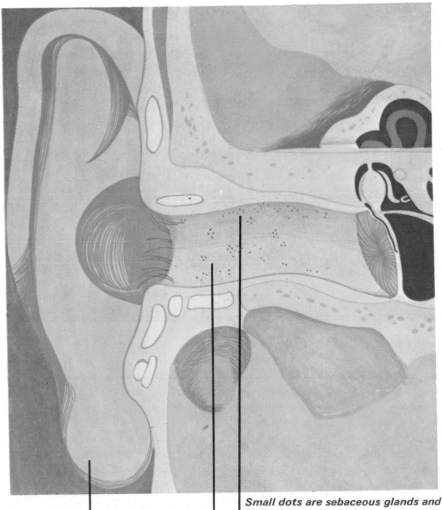

*Auricle | Meatus or ear hole*

*Small dots are sebaceous glands and ceruminous glands*

ur ears? **WHY** do babies cry so much?

## BABY CRYING

Because a baby is unable to put its feelings and desires into words it communicates vocally with other people by crying. Crying in a baby is by no means only associated with unhappy experiences, such as being hungry or feeling unwell and tears do not normally appear unless the baby is really distressed.

Most mothers get to know the "vocabulary" of cries used by their baby and believe that they can tell with some accuracy what it wants from the nature of its cry. For instance, if a baby is hungry it will most likely continue to cry if picked up, but if it is crying from boredom it will stop crying when picked up or when moved to other, more interesting, surroundings.

Of course, it is not always possible to know why a baby cries. There are occasions when it is neither hungry, tired, uncomfortable, bored, frightened or wanting to be cuddled and a mother finds it impossible to quieten the baby's cries. Neither, it would seem, does the baby know what it wants and so it cries!

# WHY do we have bones? WHY should we wash our hand

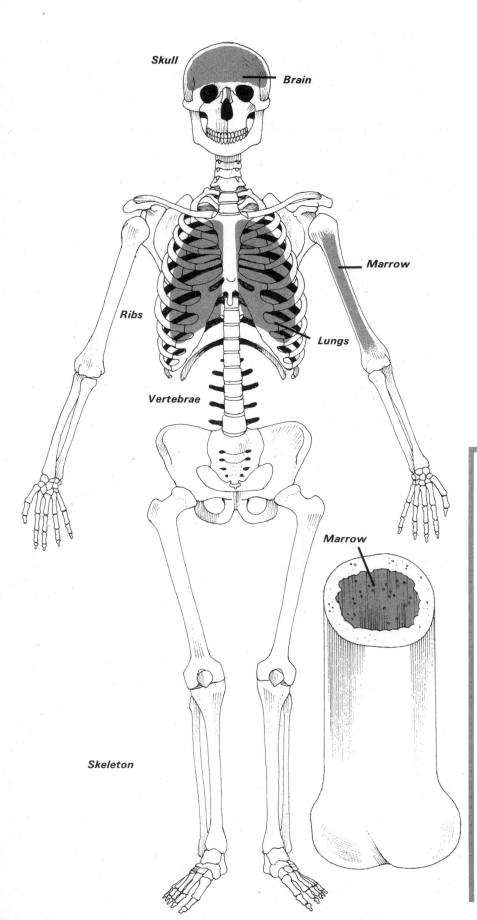

Skull

Brain

Marrow

Ribs

Lungs

Vertebrae

Marrow

Skeleton

## BONES

We have bones to give us shape and support the body, to protect and contain the body's delicate vital organs, and to help us move about.

Bones are made from living tissue, composed of special cells which secrete around themselves hard material rich in calcium salts. In a child the bones are soft and cartilaginous (Cartilage is gristle, the elastic substance of the ear or nose). Bone-making, or ossification, is a gradual process. A baby has as many as 270 bones, but an adult only 206, for some bones grow together as they get older.

All bones have a middle cavity filled with a yellow or red fatty substance called bone marrow, the blood-making factory of the body, which also keeps bones light without reducing their strength.

## WASHING HANDS

We should wash our hands before meals as a protection against infections. We live in a world full of germs (micro-organisms or microbes) and those which are dangerous to us prefer to live and multiply in organic material. So it is wise to remove as many as possible before coming into contact with food, which provides an ideal breeding ground.

Most of what are commonly called germs are harmless and some are even beneficial. Others, which are called pathogenic (disease producing), invade the body and live by feeding off body tissues.

Bacteria, which are tiny single-celled organisms, cause diseases such as diphtheria, cholera, leprosy, whooping-cough, typhoid fever, tetanus and scarlet fever, etc. Viruses are so small that scientists can see them only under immensely powerful electron microscopes. Yet they are responsible for an enormous range of human

efore meals? **WHY** are wisdom teeth so called?
**WHY** do men have an "Adam's apple"?

The basic part of the skeleton is the spine, which has 33 bones or vertebrae. The spine carries the weight of the body, is extremely flexible and contains and protects the delicate spinal cord. The skull shelters the brain while the ribs protect the heart and lungs.

Bones fit together at the joints and are held firm by ligaments, which are made of tough tissue like cords or straps. Inside each joint is a thin membraneous bag which secretes a lubricant to make the joint move smoothly.

Some glide on one another, as the lower jaw slides on the upper. Some, such as the elbow and the knee, hinge on each other and others, like the hip, make a ball and socket joint. Bones are sometimes fused together and immovable, as in the five large, lower vertebrae called the sacrum.

diseases, from colds to rabies.

In hospitals, antisepsis and asepsis are used to maintain standards of hygiene. Antisepsis aims to destroy germs already present in a wound by applying chemicals. Asepsis keeps the germs away from wounds through the sterilization of the surgeon's hands, instruments, dressings and every other possible source of any infection.

The antiseptic system was introduced into surgery by Lord Lister (1827–1912), who worked on the discoveries of the French scientist Louis Pasteur (1822–95). At first he used pure carbolic acid, which was too strong and often damaged human tissue. Then better disinfectants were discovered.

The method of asepsis began with the sterilization of instruments by superheated steam. Penicillin and other new drugs have made the control of germs much less difficult.

## WISDOM TEETH

Wisdom teeth are so called because they do not usually appear until the age of 18 to 20, by which time people were supposed to have become wiser. But surveys have shown that at least 19 per cent of the population of central Europe have failed to cut one or more wisdom teeth.

These teeth are the third molars and help in the process of grinding and chewing food. There should be four of them right at the back of the mouth next to eight other molars. Nearer the centre of the mouth are the eight bicuspids (or premolars) followed by the four cuspids (or canines) which are used for cutting and tearing food.

The eight front teeth, or incisors, are used mainly for biting and cutting, while the upper ones enable them to identify objects by nibbling.

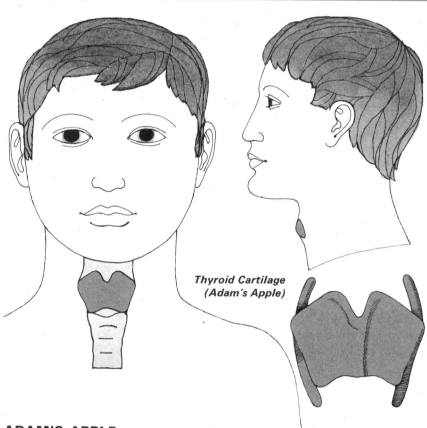

*Thyroid Cartilage (Adam's Apple)*

## ADAM'S APPLE

An "Adam's apple" is to be found in both men and women and is part of the larynx, or "voice box", situated at the top of the windpipe in front of the neck. The larynx is a more or less rigid box created by a framework of cartilages connected by ligaments. The most important of these cartilages is the thyroid forming the prominence called "Adam's apple". The others are the cricoid cartilage and the epiglottis. The vocal cords are suspended in the larynx. These are two fibrous bands which are anchored fore and aft.

The chords are heavier and thicker in man than in woman, which makes the thyroid cartilage more pronounced. This led in olden times to the wrong belief that the "Adam's apple" was only to be found in man. The term itself arises from the ancient belief that it marks the place where the apple given by Eve to Adam got stuck!

## RESEMBLING PARENTS

We resemble our parents because of a complex of biological processes which we call heredity. Parents and children tend to be similar in many characteristics—structural, physiological and psychological. However, the young are not exact duplicates of their parents and usually differ in many traits. This difference we call variation.

The science of the study of heredity is called genetics, and the most famous name connected with it is that of Gregor Johann Mendel (1822–1884), an Austrian monk whose discoveries laid the foundation of the science.

Mendel studied plants, especially the garden pea, and showed that inherited characteristics were the result of paired elementary units of heredity, which we now call genes. These he symbolized by letters. A characteristic of one parent, such as tallness, which appeared in the progeny to the exclusion of another, was said to be dominant. A characteristic which tended not to reappear was called recessive.

Later studies have shown that the genes are carried by structures called chromosomes. The human body begins with the union of two sex cells, and the body of a new-born infant has some 200,000 million cells. These cells arise through the division of other cells. When they divide, their nuclei (or tiny central bodies) divide also by a remarkable process called mitosis.

During mitosis the nuclei resolve themselves into structures called chromosomes, which divide lengthwise. All body cells have true copies of all chromosomes that were present in the fertilized egg from which the body developed.

*This detail from the famous painting by Goya shows the striking resemblance of the family to Charles IV of Spain.*

## TEMPERATURE

The body temperature of a human being is an indication of his physical condition, so that an abnormally high or low temperature is generally a sign that something is wrong.

The normal temperature is usually given as 36·9°C. (98·4°F.), but as the body temperature varies throughout the day, anything between 36·9°C. (or lower) and 37·5°C. (or 99·5°F.) may be taken, for all practical purposes, as normal.

For instance, the temperature rises after a large meal, during hot weather and after violent exercise. Your temperature is at its lowest at night when you are asleep.

Control of body temperature is exercised by a centre in the brain which ensures that a balance exists between heat production and heat loss. A raised temperature is often the sign of bacterial or virus infection. It may be due to heatstroke, to certain types of brain injury or disease or to shock.

A very high temperature, or fever, may begin with a "rigor" (an attack of shivering and cold), in which the whole body may tremble uncontrollably and the teeth chatter. Although at this stage the skin feels cold and clammy, the temperature within the body is raised. Soon the skin becomes hot and dry, pulse and breathing rate are speeded up and there is a feeling of exhaustion, aching muscles, headache, thirst and perhaps delirium and loss of the sense of time.

Finally this stage is succeeded by profuse sweating and a gradual relief of the symptoms.

our temperature if he thinks you are unwell?

# WHY do we have two eyes?　WHY do you get "pins an

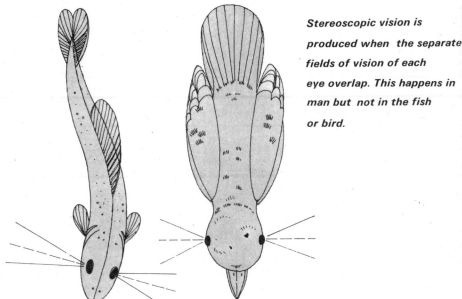

*Stereoscopic vision is produced when the separate fields of vision of each eye overlap. This happens in man but not in the fish or bird.*

## TWO EYES

We have two eyes placed in the front of our heads because we need to be able to judge distances and to see in depth. The change in the position of the eyes from the side of the head in our remote ancestors probably came about because they needed to be able to judge distances accurately as they swung from branch to branch in the trees.

With both eyes in front, their separate fields of vision overlap. We see two images superimposed one upon the other but, because of the space between our eyes, the image from each goes a little way around its own side of the object. This is called stereoscopic vision, or vision in depth, which we share with apes and monkeys. Most other animals and fish do not have

this advantage. To them the world appears flat. One exception is the owl, who sees better than any of us, and has not only stereoscopic vision, but telescopic vision, too.

Our judgement of distance depends, with near objects, upon our stereoscopic vision. As the distance increases, there is less difference between the left-eyed and the right-eyed view. So we depend upon other factors as well.

Experience tells us that the farther away an object is, the smaller it looks. Its colour also changes, its details disappear, its outline softens. Nearer objects give us a measure against which to judge the distance of farther ones. Then there is perspective, the familiar illusion that parallel lines converge towards the horizon.

## BRAIN

The brain directs and coordinates movements and reflexes, registers sensations and is the supreme nervous organ by which man acquires knowledge and the power to use and adapt it. It shapes our personalities, and without it we would be more helpless than the tiniest human baby.

There are three main parts of the brain: the forebrain (or cerebrum), the midbrain and the hindbrain. They have the consistency of soft jelly and are protected by three membranes (meninges), a tough outer envelope called the dura and a watery fluid (cerebrospinal fluid) which acts as a support and a cushion. The brain is connected to the spinal cord, and its surface is highly convoluted.

## PINS AND NEEDLES

"Pins and needles" is the name given to a tingling sensation you feel in your hands, feet, arms or legs when the blood begins to circulate again in those areas after being impeded. When you sit with one leg doubled up underneath you, you probably find when you try to stand, that your leg has "fallen asleep" and is numb. As

the blood begins to flow again, the familiar tingling sensation will occur.

Blood has been called "the river of life" and its circulation both distributes supplies to the body's cells and removes their waste. The body's five quarts of blood make a complete circuit of the system once every minute.

Without this the cells would cease to function.

A tourniquet, a tie round a limb to halt the circulation, is sometimes used to stop bleeding from a wound into a vein or artery. But a tourniquet is generally loosened every 30 minutes and it should not be kept on for more than two hours at a time.

eedles"? WHY do we have a brain? WHY do we sleep? WHY does hair grow when a person dies?

## SLEEP

Some scientists consider that sleep is an instinct, a basic need for the body and mind to relax and to escape from the responses needed while awake. We become tired in body and mind if we do not sleep, and scientists have proved that when we do sleep the electrical activity of the brain slows down, although it may be stimulated when we dream.

One chemical theory is that a substance needed to maintain the waking state becomes exhausted and may be replenished in sleep. A contrary suggestion is that some poisonous substances built up in wakefulness may be destroyed when we go to sleep.

Other theories connect the need for increased wakefulness with the development of the more sophisticated areas of the brain. This could explain why new-born babies whose powers of reasoning have not yet developed, spend most of their lives asleep. It has been demonstrated that a particular part of the brain, the reticular formation, if severed, causes continuous sleep.

Although we are not sure why we sleep, there is no doubt that we need to do so and so do most other animals. The pattern of sleep and wakefulness is closely associated with our habits and senses.

Animals which depend upon sight for food, shelter and defence, like man, are diurnal. That means they are for the most part active during the day and sleep at night.

The amount of sleep needed by a person to remain in full health varies considerably with age, with different individuals, and even, perhaps, with race. Pre-school children generally need ten to twelve hours sleep, schoolchildren nine to eleven hours and adults seven to nine hours. Adults seem to need progressively less sleep as they grow older, and exceptional cases are known of elderly people who have remained healthy on two to three hours a night. It has been said that the Japanese, both children and adults, sleep less than Europeans, but that may be due to habit rather than to race.

The cerebrum, which forms nearly nine-tenths of the brain, is divided into two halves (hemispheres). Generally the left half of the cerebrum controls the right half of the body, and the right half of the cerebrum controls the left half of the body. Some areas are connected with the special senses of man, but there are so-called "silent areas" which scientists believe are connected with memory and the association of ideas. The thalamus, a mass of grey matter which is buried in the cerebrum, is the source of instinctive feeling and emotion.

The midbrain is concerned with eye-movements, while the hindbrain contains the nerve cells responsible for breathing, heart action, digestive juices and so on. The cerebellum, a part of the hindbrain, plays an important role in the execution of the more highly skilled movements.

## HAIR

Hair goes on growing after a person dies because the cells of the body go on working until they have exhausted their fuel supply.

Human cells have been described as power plants, chemical laboratories, furnaces and factories. They are marvellous structures, which carry out the functions for which they have been designed with great efficiency.

The hair follicle is composed of two layers—an outer layer of cells forming the outer root sheath and an inner horny layer of horny, fibrous oblong cells. The hair grows upwards from the bottom of the follicle by multiplication of the soft cells, which become elongated and pigmented to form the fibre-like substance of the hair shaft.

The soft cells at the base of the follicle need the nourishment brought to them and all the other cells of the body by the blood-stream.

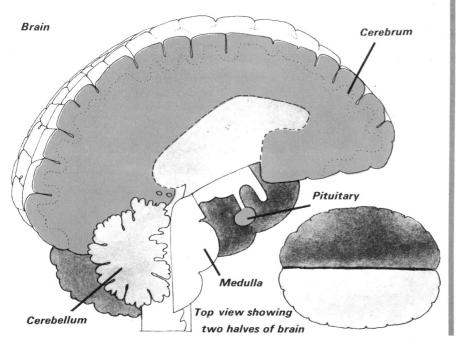

Brain

Cerebrum

Pituitary

Medulla

Cerebellum

Top view showing two halves of brain

# Science and Technology

### FERTILIZERS

Fertilizers are used on farms to increase crop yields by ensuring that soils contain the chemical elements required by growing plants. These chemical elements include oxygen, carbon, hydrogen, nitrogen, phosphorous, potassium, sulphur, calcium, magnesium, and iron. If soils are lacking in any of these, the deficiency can be made good by the right fertilizer.

Until the 19th Century, farmers relied mainly on the application of natural fertilizers to put "goodness" back into the land. They used manure from the stock-yards and, in the case of coastal areas, sea-weed from the shore. Lime was also applied to prevent acidity. This method of soil rejuvenation went a long way to maintain the presence of chemical elements. But it often did little to improve soils already lacking in certain chemicals.

Nowadays soils are analysed to find out deficiencies which can be made up by the application of the appropriate chemical fertilizers. Of course, the chemicals alone do not guarantee a successful crop. The continued application of the natural fertilizers, such as manure and humus (decayed vegetable matter) is also essential.

### OIL AND WATER

Oil and water do not mix because the molecules (tiny particles) of which they are composed are so different. The molecules in oil are much bigger and contain many more atoms than those of water.

When different liquids mix, it is because they have similar types of molecules which readily link up with each other, like milk and water. In the case of oil and water the groups of molecules prefer to stay apart.

The patches of oil floating on top of the water are usually circular because of another characteristic of molecules, which produces what scientists term surface tension. This is a cohesive force caused by the attraction of the molecules to each other. They cling so tightly that they produce a surface layer which acts like an elastic skin or the rubber envelope of a balloon. The molecules are trying to pull the liquid into as small a space as possible. As well as producing a circular shape, this tension makes the surface area of each oil patch as small as possible.

### CARBURETTOR

An automobile is driven by an internal combustion engine which will work properly only if the right amounts of petrol and air are mixed together. The carburettor is the part of the engine where the mixing takes place.

The burning of fuel in the engine is a chemical reaction in which petrol combines with the oxygen of the air to produce water, heat energy and oxides of carbon. A chemically correct mixture should have 15 parts of air to one part of petrol, both by weight. The amount of air then present is just sufficient to burn the petrol com-

on a farm? WHY does an automobile have a carburettor?
WHY are ice-skates made of steel?

## ICE-SKATES

Ice-skate blades are made of steel for three reasons. First, because steel is immensely strong, hard and resistant to wear. Second, because it is a relatively low conductor of heat. And third, because it can be sharpened to a keen edge.

A skate blade has to resist tremendous pressure because it is hollow-ground, so that only the edges rest on the ice.

The smooth gliding movement associated with skating is made possible by a thin film of water on the ice produced by heat friction as the blade strikes the surface. As it is a relatively poor conductor of heat, the steel allows the heat to remain for a longer time at the edge of the blade, thus ensuring the necessary film of water.

There are specially designed blades for different kinds of ice-skating. The figure skater's blade is hollow ground and curved with saw-like teeth at the toe to enable the skater to get a better grip on the ice when carrying out certain movements. The speed skater uses a thinner blade, about 16–17 inches long, sharpened, with a flat surface. This type of blade gives the racer a longer stroke.

pletely. If the engine uses a mixture with an excess of petrol—a rich mixture—a small amount of unburnt petrol will be present in the exhaust fumes.

A carburettor has to produce the required mixture in varying strengths to suit different engine conditions, such as starting, idling, acceleration, cruising and application of full power. It must be able to pass the correct mixture at all engine speeds and under varying loads, and has to atomize the petrol into tiny droplets and vaporize the resulting spray into a combustible mixture.

Inside the carburettor is a throttle valve which can increase or decrease the amount of mixture passing into the cylinders, which in turn controls the power of the engine. This valve is mounted on a spindle which is operated by the accelerator pedal.

A special device called a "strangler" is also incorporated to help in starting the engine in cold weather by allowing an extra-rich mixture. This is commonly referred to as the choke.

*The diagram shows the principle of the carburettor.*

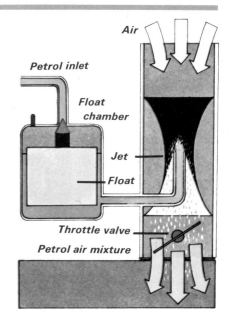

Air

Petrol inlet

Float chamber

Jet

Float

Throttle valve

Petrol air mixture

# WHY do some acids burn? WHY do objects appear reversed

## ACIDS

Some acids burn because they have a strong tendency to absorb water, giving out a great deal of heat in the process. Since most living cells contain water the strong acids, such as sulphuric acid, hydrochloric acid and nitric acid, react with them and kill the cells, causing very serious burns.

These three acids, as well as others such as perchloric acid and benzine sulphuric acid are called mineral acids because they are manufactured from minerals. They are all strong and dangerous acids. They have tremendous industrial value, but great care must be used in handling them.

Most organic acids—that is to say, those made from living things—are weak acids. Vinegar or lemon juice are examples. All acids taste sour and most attack metals, turning them into salts and releasing hydrogen.

Special clothing is worn by men handling acids to protect them from serious burns. Acid must always be poured *slowly* into water, never water into acid. If you are burned by acid you should wash your skin with large quantities of water and then with a weak ammonia solution. If your eyes are affected, flush them immediately with lots of water and then with bicarbonate of soda solution, which neutralizes any acid left.

## ASTRONAUT

A space suit enables an astronaut to survive by providing him artificially with conditions like those he is used to on earth.

These conditions can be reproduced in a large space craft or space station in orbit, but an astronaut still needs a space suit for operations outside the craft or for an emergency.

In space men lack the air needed for breathing, the pressure required to stop their blood from boiling and the natural protection of the atmosphere against radiation. All these must be supplied by the space suit which also must withstand the cold of space.

When an astronaut ventures into space, he leaves behind the safety of the atmospheric blanket which we, on earth, take for granted. His space suit becomes his own personal little world.

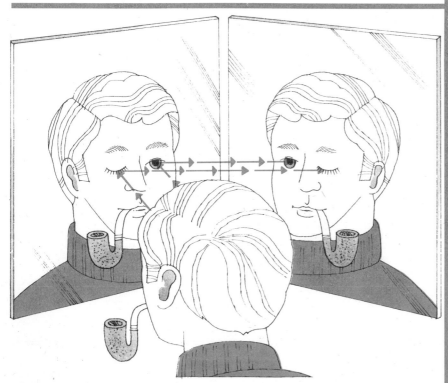

## MIRROR

Objects will appear reversed in a mirror because what you are seeing is a reflection and not a reproduction of the image. If you stand in front of a mirror with your right eye closed the image in the mirror will appear to show your left eye closed, because the image is facing the opposite direction. In all reflections images and directions are reversed.

By using a combination of two mirrors at right angles to each other, the reversal will be eliminated. This is because the reversed image will be reversed yet again in the second mirror, thus giving a true likeness of the original object.

n a mirror? **WHY** does an astronaut need a space suit?
**WHY** are there different types of saw?

## DIFFERENT SAWS

Saws are of many shapes and sizes, according to the special purposes for which they are to be used and the materials they are meant to cut. Most are designed to cut through wood but others have the particular qualities needed for cutting metals and stones.

There are two types of large hand-saw. Both have steel blades with wooden handles, but the teeth are shaped differently to fit the job they have to do. One is a cross-cut saw for cutting *across* the grain of the wood. The leading edges of the teeth slope backward and are also bevelled, or angled, transversely. In other words, they are cut away at the edges to give an oblique angle like the edge of a chisel, thus producing a sharp-pointed profile or shape designed to avoid splintering the wood.

The second type is the rip or tenon saw, which is used for cutting *along* the grain of the wood. This has a smaller blade, strengthened by a steel strip along the top edge, and smaller teeth. It is used, as the name suggests, in cutting tenon or slotted joints.

Smaller hand saws, like the fretsaw, are used for cutting intricate shapes. These have a narrow blade stretched across an open frame. The hacksaw, which is used for cutting metal by hand, also has an open frame, but its blade is deeper and more closely-toothed.

Machine saws are of three types: first, a larger and stronger hacksaw operated by an electric motor through a crank and connecting rod; second, a circular saw, which has a rotating, disc-shaped blade with teeth on the circumference; and third, a bandsaw which has a blade formed like an endless flexible band and tightly stretched over pulleys.

The bandsaw, which has fine teeth along one edge, operates at a higher speed than the circular saw. It can cut round curves of quite small radius because the blade is so narrow.

For stone-cutting in quarrying there are swinging gang-saws with teeth like chisels and flat-bladed circular saws, which are either fed with a mixture of hard sand and water or fitted with rims of a hard abrasive substance called carborundum.

The hand-held power saw driven by an electric or petrol driven engine is used for felling trees and cutting logs. This is also known as a chain-saw because it is much like a bicycle chain equipped with saw teeth.

*1. Combination: large teeth for general cutting.*

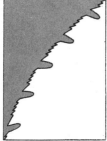
*2. Planer: hollow ground gives smooth finish.*

*3. Crosscut: to cut across the grain of the wood.*

*4. Friction: for corrugated materials and thin metals.*

## POLLUTION

Pollution is a problem because man, in an ever-increasingly populated and industrialized world, is upsetting the environment in which he lives. Many scientists maintain that one of man's greatest errors has been to equate growth with advancement. Now "growth" industries are being looked on with suspicion in case their side effects damage the environment and disrupt the relationship of different forms of life.

The growing population makes increasing demands on the world's fixed supply of air, water and land. This rise in population is accompanied by the desire of more and more people for a better standard of living. Thus still greater demands for electricity, water and goods result in an ever increasing amount of waste material to be disposed of.

The problem has been causing increasing concern to living things and their environment. Many believe that man is not solving these problems quickly enough and that his selfish pursuit of possessions take him past the point of no return before he fully appreciates the damage. It would then be too late to reverse the process.

Ecologists say we are so determined to possess a new car or washing machine, or to obtain a greater yield from our crops by the use of fertilizers, that we ignore the fact that life depends on a lot of micro-organisms working efficiently.

For example, if new chemicals were released into the environment, a combination of them might well poison one or more of the different types of bacteria in soil and water, which are essential to keep nitrogen being circulated from the air into organic material, and being cycled back into the air again. If this should happen on a world-wide scale, the air would become unbreathable.

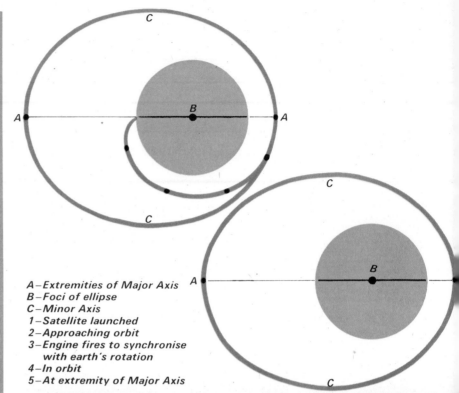

A—Extremities of Major Axis
B—Foci of ellipse
C—Minor Axis
1—Satellite launched
2—Approaching orbit
3—Engine fires to synchronise
   with earth's rotation
4—In orbit
5—At extremity of Major Axis

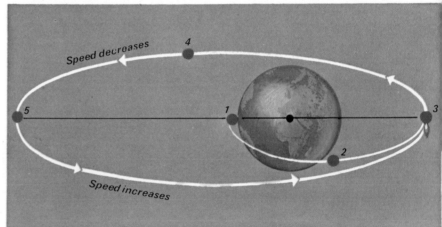

## SATELLITE

An artificial satellite remains in its regular course around the earth even after its motors have been turned off. This is not because the satellite has been lifted beyond the reach of gravity but because its centrifugal force just balances the gravitational pull of the earth.

Launching a satellite calls for a propellant, such as a rocket which can move it high enough and fast enough to make it orbit the earth at a constant height indefinitely. There is no air in space to slow it down.

Since the pull of gravity grows less as the distance from the earth's surface increases, the speed required—its orbital velocity—also grows less.

At a height of 200 miles the orbital speed required is 17,200 m.p.h. At about 22,000 miles, the required speed would cause the satellite to take 24 hours to complete an orbit. It would thus rotate with the earth and maintain a fixed position above it.

n orbit?  WHY were the Galapagos Islands important
to Charles Darwin?

*Above: A Galapagos iguana.*

## GALAPAGOS ISLANDS

In 1831 Charles Darwin sailed in H.M.S. Beagle on an expedition which would take him to the Galapagos Islands. On arrival he was so impressed by the animal life that the islands inspired many of his ideas on evolution, in particular his monumental work *The Origin of Species.*

Here he had proof for his views on natural selection. In front of his eyes were albatross and cormorant that could not fly, and giant land tortoises weighing over 500 pounds and considered among the oldest living creatures on earth.

There were also such extraordinary curiosities as a four-eyed fish and tame finches which would use sticks as tools to obtain food. Also, Darwin discovered a species of penguin unlike any others and large spiny iguanas, the only lizards that take to water.

The Galapagos Islands are in the Pacific Ocean, off the coasts of Ecuador and Peru, in South America.

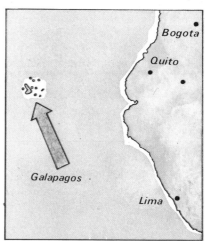

**WHY** is uranium important?    **WHY** do motor vehicles have
**WHY** do some liquids burn?    **WHY** are some

## URANIUM

The importance of uranium today lies in its value as a producer of nuclear power. Uranium was first discovered by the German chemist, Martin Klaproth in 1789. But for a century and a half afterwards few uses could be found for the new metallic element.

Some suggested making filaments for lamps out of it. Uranium has actually been used success-fully in large lamps for photo-graphy. Also, it was of some value as a dye for wood and leather.

In 1938, two scientists, Hahn and Strassmann, discovered that uranium could yield nuclear energy. One pound of uranium would give as much energy as three million pounds of coal. The first nuclear chain reaction was conducted by Enrico Fermi in 1942. This made possible the exploding of the first atomic bomb in 1945.

Apart from its destructive ap-plications, the use of uranium in nuclear power stations has proved a valuable substitute for the world's dwindling supply of oil and coal. Also, isotopes extracted from uranium have proved immensely useful in medicine by helping to diagnose and treat illnesses.

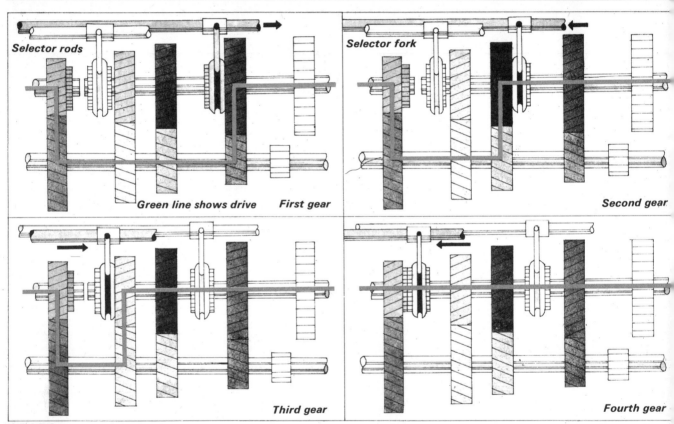

Selector rods

Green line shows drive    First gear

Selector fork

Second gear

Third gear

Fourth gear

## GEARS

A transmission gear system is used in motor vehicles because petrol engines have little power at low speeds. So to make the vehicle move off or climb a hill the engine has to turn fast while the wheels are revolving slowly. The gears provide the means of altering the ratio between the speed of the engine and the speed of the wheels.

The gear box is so arranged that the driver can link the engine shaft to the transmission through large to small gears for the vehicle to move faster, or through small to large gears for it to move more slowly. Some of the gears are fixed to the shafts while others can be slid along the shafts but they will still turn when the shafts revolve.

With the gear lever, various combinations of these gear wheels can be brought into action. These combinations give first—or bottom —gear for slow speeds up to, say, 20 miles per hour, and two, three or four more up to top gear for speeds of 65 m.p.h. and over. On some vehicles an extra high gear is incorporated by means of a device called an overdrive. This is a great advantage for long runs since it reduces engine speed by 22 per cent for any given road speed, thereby reducing petrol consumption and engine wear.

Many motor vehicles are fitted with automatic gear boxes which adjust engine speed in correct relation to road speed without the driver having to change gear.

gears? **WHY** do people study cybernetics?

metals chromium-plated? **WHY** are tuning-forks used?

## CYBERNETICS

People study cybernetics to gain knowledge with which to improve mechanical things. Cybernetics is the scientific study of automatic control and communication in the functions of animals and in mechanical and electrical systems. It is chiefly concerned with physiological and psychological mechanics of animal behaviour.

These methods have been used in deciphering garbled messages, in anti-aircraft gunnery, in constructing artificial limbs, in building computers and in making models of the human brain.

Cybernetics comes from the Greek *kubernetes* meaning steersman. It is a word much in vogue among engineers.

## LIQUIDS THAT BURN

Some liquids will burn because when their molecules mix with the oxygen in the air the mixture becomes combustible.

The application of heat promotes the necessary chemical reaction to put the molecules into more violent motion, so that they collide at high speed. The jolt loosens the bonds and makes it easier for the molecules to rearrange themselves and escape from the liquid to form a vapour, mixing with oxygen in the air.

The most important liquid which will burn is crude mineral oil from which petrol and paraffin are produced. Others include tar and creosote, and the very explosive nitro-glycerine.

## TUNING-FORKS

A tuning-fork vibrates to give a musical note of definite pitch or frequency and is marked on the fork by a letter or symbol referring to its position in the musical scale.

The instrument has two hard steel prongs and a handle or stem. It is sounded by giving one of the prongs a light tap on a wooden surface, and then holding the handle on a wooden board or table.

Tuning-forks are used by piano-tuners and musicians. Most forks give the same musical note as Middle C on a piano and are usually marked 256. The number gives the frequency and means that it vibrates at a rate of 256 times a second. In 1939 a frequency of 440 for A was agreed.

## CHROMIUM PLATE

Some metals are chromium-plated to make them look more attractive and to prevent them from corroding or rusting. Chromium is a silver-white, hard, brittle metal which was discovered in 1798 by N. L. Vauquelin. Its non-corrosive, high-strength, heat-resistant characteristics are utilized in alloys and as an electroplated coating.

In electroplating, the article to be plated is connected to the negative terminal of a battery and placed in a solution known as electrolyte. Direct electric current is introduced through the anode or positive terminal, which usually consists of the metal with which the article is to be coated. Metal dissolves from the anode and forms a deposit on the article. The electrolyte for chromium contains chromic acid and sulphuric acid. It deposits a bright top layer but this is not the most important part of the electroplating. The chromium is only about 0·00002 inches thick. Under it lies a thick layer of nickel and beneath that again may be a layer of copper.

Many household appliances are chromium-plated and so are the bright parts of an automobile. Tools, chemical equipment, electric appliances, gears, packing machinery, and hundreds of other articles are similarly treated to give them brightness, beauty or resistance to wear and rust. Electroplated and polished chromium is bright bluish-white with a reflecting power which is 77 per cent that of silver.

# WHY does iron go red when heated? WHY does a magnifyin
# WHY is a diesel engine more efficient than the petrol engine

## IRON

Iron goes red when heated because its atoms radiate vibratory waves of an electrodynamic nature which are visible as light at a sufficiently high temperature. At 800° Centigrade the iron is at low-red heat. But as the heat increases the iron will turn bright red, and finally white-hot and molten.

Heat is passed through the iron by conduction—the contact of one iron particle with another with no visible movement of the particles. The heat which is given off as light when iron glows red-hot can be reconverted into heat by the substance on to which it falls. When iron is heated to a temperature below 300° Centigrade it gives off invisible rays of infra-red radiation which are similar in nature to light. But they do not contain quite enough energy per unit (photon) to stimulate the optic nerve and so be seen by the human eye.

## MAGNIFYING GLASS

A magnifying glass consists of a double-convex lens which bends the rays of light that pass through it and so makes objects appear larger. This bending of the light rays deceives our eyes. We do not see the actual object we are looking at, but rays of light from the direction from which they would come if we were looking at a much bigger object.

A convex lens is a circular piece of glass which has been ground, or shaped, so that its centre is thicker than its outside edge. A concave lens is thinner at its centre than at its outside edge, and this makes objects look smaller.

Magnifying glasses, or convex lenses, are used in telescopes and microscopes. A telescope makes distant objects appear nearer by means of two convex lenses. This can be shown by using two old spectacle lenses. The one held nearer the eyes should be thicker than the one nearer the object.

## LIGHT BULB

A light bulb gives off light because an electric current is passed through its filament, a thread of tungsten metal thinner than a human hair, which then becomes white hot.

Sir Joseph Swan (1828–1914) in England and Thomas Alva Edison (1847–1931) in the United States constructed the first incandescent electric lamps in 1879. They succeeded in preventing the rapid burning up of the filament by oxidization, but their problem lay in the choice of a suitable material for the filament.

Edison sat in his laboratory watching a filament of charred cotton thread glow in a glass bulb, which had been exhausted of air, for 40 hours. But the thread was too fragile to sustain the heat provided by the electric current. A material was needed that would stand great heat, for the hotter the filament, the brighter is the light

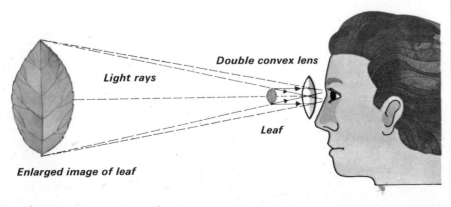

*Light rays*

*Double convex lens*

*Leaf*

*Enlarged image of leaf*

# glass magnify? WHY does an electric light bulb give off light? WHY don't cranes topple over?

## DIESEL ENGINE

The diesel engine is more efficient than the petrol engine because of its greater thermal efficiency. This means that the ratio of the work done by the engine to the amount of heat supplied is higher. Since the heat in this case comes from fuel-oil, it is not possible to convert all the heat energy in the fuel into useful work. There are losses due to friction, exhaust and radiation.

The compression-ignition, or diesel engine was invented by the German engineer Rudolf Diesel in 1897. It is much simpler in construction than the petrol, or spark-ignition engine. Pre-ignition troubles are avoided because only the air in the engine cylinder is compressed and the fuel is introduced only at the instant of combustion. The engine requires no spark-plugs and burns fuel-oil which is less expensive than petrol.

The basic construction of the diesel engine is similar to the petrol engine. The main difference is the way in which the fuel is introduced and ignited. With an average compression ratio of 16:1 the air in the cylinder during the compression stroke reaches a pressure of about 500 pounds a square inch.

At the right instant a precise amount of fuel passes from the injector pump to the injector at high pressure and enters the cylinder as a fine spray. Owing to the high temperature of the air, the fuel starts to burn without the need for a spark.

But the high pressure means that diesel engines have to be stronger than petrol engines. They are, therefore, heavier and more expensive.

## CRANES

Cranes do not topple over because their jibs or booms are counterbalanced at the opposite end from the lifted load, thus keeping the centre of gravity over the base.

The first cranes were simply long poles fixed in the ground at an angle, with a pulley at the top through which passed a rope. They were called "cranes" because they looked rather like the neck of the bird with the same name.

The derrick crane, which looks like a gallows, is named after Dick Derrick, a 17th Century hangman. In the middle of the 18th Century, steam engines began to be used on cranes, while today the lifting may be done by varieties of power.

Jib cranes may be portable, being mounted on a wheeled carriage, or they may be self-propelled. Gantry cranes with long booms are used for unloading ships while overhead cranes are used in factories. Goliath cranes, with steel towers at either side, capable of lifting 200 tons are used at some atomic power stations.

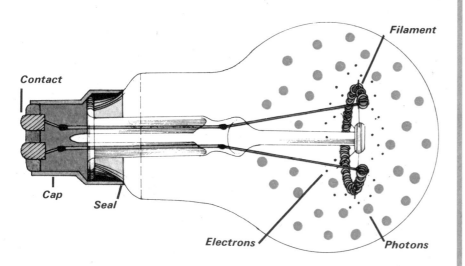

given by the lamp.

But even with the present day use of tungsten, the problem still remains in that the more a filament is heated, the sooner it will burn away. To solve this problem, gas discharge lamps were invented. These consist of glass tubes filled with sodium or mercury vapour, or neon gas. At each end of the tubes are electrodes, or contacts. When an electric current is applied to one of the contacts it passes through the gas to the other contact, causing the gas to glow and give out light.

# WHY is Einstein famous?   WHY does a motor vehicle need

# WHY is radioactivity dangerous?   WHY is a convector heate

## EINSTEIN

Albert Einstein is famous for his Theories of Relativity which say that nothing in the universe is absolutely still and that all motion is connected or comparable. Einstein worked out a method of measuring the speed of moving objects, using the three dimensions of space—length, height and thickness—and adding the fourth dimension of time. The three space dimensions tell us where the object is, while the fourth tells us when.

In the relativity theories the movement of any object is represented by lines, called "world-lines", with the dimensions of time and space—as a four-dimensional graph. If an object moves with uniform speed and in a straight line, its world-line will be straight. If it moves under the force of gravity, such as a falling stone, it will drop not at a uniform pace, but at an increasing speed. So its world-line will be a curve.

Einstein was born in 1879 at Ulm in Germany of German-Jewish parents. He published his first paper on the Special Theory of Relativity in 1905, his second paper on the General Theory of Relativity ten years later. In 1921 he was awarded the Nobel Prize for Physics. In 1950 he published another paper, an extension to the General Theory designed to include magnetism and electricity and called the Unified Field Theory.

His remarkable ability as a scientist did not stop him from taking a keen interest in other affairs, and he held passionate views on peace and world unity. He was also an accomplished violinist.

In 1952, three years before his death, he rejected a suggestion that he should be nominated to be President of Israel.

## RADIOACTIVITY

Radioactivity is dangerous because it can expose people to a harmful dose of radiation even without being aware of it. A number of small doses received over a very long time could lead to leukaemia or cancer in later life.

Radiation can lead to the retention of a potentially harmful amount of radium in one's bones. Radioactivity resulting from nuclear bomb tests can cause ingenuous quantities of radio-strontium and radiocaesium to get into food.

A radium compound was once used in the manufacture of luminous paint for the numbers on clocks, watches and instrument dials. The girls who painted these had a habit of putting the brush in their mouths to get a fine pointed tip. In those days the danger was not realized, and, over a long period, many workers absorbed enough radium to cause death in later years.

## CONVECTOR HEATER

Heating appliances specially designed to create a circulating movement of warmed air are called convection heaters because they use convection currents of air.

When air is heated it becomes less dense and, since warm air is lighter than cold air it duly rises and is replaced by cold air.

Convector heaters consist, basically, of metal cabinets with openings at the top and bottom to produce and direct this flow of rising warm air. At the base of this cabinet there is a heating element and this warms the air within the cabinet.

This warm air rises and, as it rises, cold air is drawn into the convector from the bottom of the appliance. The cabinet of the convector acts as a flue or chimney and creates a continuous current of warm air.

## MOTOR OIL

Every moving part of a motor vehicle engine needs lubrication. Oil provides this lubrication, without which much of the power generated by the engine would be wasted through friction.

Lubrication creates a protective film between all those parts of the engine that rub together. This minimizes wear, and prevents breakages and possible fire. Oil also reduces noise and stops the engine from overheating too easily, by cooling the working parts.

An engine that is regularly oiled will automatically be clean. The oil acts as a detergent and prevents rust.

il? **WHY** do aircraft break the sound barrier with a bang?
so called? **WHY** can transistor radio valves be so small?

*Path of double sonic boom*

## SOUND BARRIER

The loud double bangs produced when aircraft break the sound barrier are caused by shock waves from the plane's wings.

An aircraft travelling at a speed less than that of sound produces waves which travel ahead of it. At this speed the waves seem to prepare the way for the machine, so that the air slides over and under the wing surfaces easily.

As the plane approaches the speed of sound, the waves travel at the same speed as the machine and the air tends to swirl and break unevenly over the wing surfaces.

At the speed of sound shock waves are projected outwards and backwards from the leading and trailing edges of the aircraft. These waves are heard as two quick loud claps like thunder and are usually followed by a somewhat diminished roar as the aircraft breaks through the sound barrier.

## TRANSISTOR

Transistor radio valves can be small because they are made with a class of material called semi-conductors.

In the early days of radio it was essential to have a rectifier, a component which allowed an electric current to flow with a low resistance in one direction and a high resistance in the opposite direction. This involved the use of a piece of carborundum crystal and a steel point.

Then a diode-valve was used as a rectifier. This consisted of two separated metals in a vacuum. They were contained in a thin glass tube, two inches long and one inch in diameter. More progress was made by the discovery of materials with an electrical resistance between high-value insulators and low-value substances such as plastic and copper. Two such materials, now widely used in industry and called semi-conductors, are silicon, a non-metallic

element and germanium, a metallic element.

Only a small amount of the elements is required and only a few volts are needed to carry the current. By a special industrial melting process, these semi-conductors can be joined together in layers like a sandwich. A transistor is basically a sandwich of three layers of semi-conductors, and it is possible to obtain several combinations.

Since the resistance of all semi-conductors is sensitive to light, the sandwich is housed in a sealed capsule and coated with black lacquer.

Transistors can be any size from a grain of rice to $\frac{1}{4}$ inch long. They can perform many of the functions of multi-electrode valves, need only a small voltage battery, are less liable to breakage, are considerably cheaper to produce and can be very much smaller.

100

# WHY do fire extinguishers stop flames?  WHY do lunar
## WHY does iron rust?  WHY is i

## FIRE EXTINGUISHERS

Fire extinguishers stop flames either by dousing them in water or by excluding the oxygen which a fire needs in order to burn.

There are three main kinds of fires. First are those occurring in ordinary materials like paper and wood for which the quenching and cooling effects of water or water solutions are the most effective. Second come those involving inflammable liquids or greases for which a blanketing or smothering effect is essential. Finally there are the fires occurring in "live" electrical equipment where a special extinguishing agent must be used.

The most common extinguisher for the first type of fire is a bucket of water, or a manufactured extinguisher with water containing a chemical. The chemical reaction expels the water which puts out the fire.

For the second kind of fire the most common method is to use a chemical extinguisher to spray the burning material with foam which puts out the fire by excluding oxygen. This foam usually consists of bubbles of carbon dioxide. As the foam is not a conductor of electricity, it may also be used safely on the third type of fire.

Foam-type extinguishers can generally be employed safely in nearly all cases, but water or water solutions should never be used on oil, grease or electrical fires.

## LUNAR MODULES

A lunar module needs a blast-off platform because it is propelled by a rocket engine.

This engine carries its own fuel and oxidizer and can, therefore, operate at great heights where little or no air is present. It can thus be used on the moon's surface where there is no air.

Very hot gases are expelled from the rear of a rocket. The engine depends for its operation on the upward thrust (on the rocket and the load carried) being equal and opposite to the downward thrust (of the burnt gases). That is why a blast-off platform is needed.

modules need a blast-off platform?

dangerous to take electrical appliances into a bathroom?

## IRON RUST

Iron rusts, or corrodes, in air because it dissolves in the acid solution provided by the moisture and the carbon dioxide of the air to form hydrous oxide. In an atmosphere which is rich in sulphur compounds—for instance, very smoky air—the process will be accelerated.

Our industrial system is largely based on the use of iron and its alloys. It is the world's most important metal, but rarely found in a pure state. Iron ore has to be smelted to separate the metal from other elements. The molten iron which flows from the blast furnace after smelting is called pig iron. This contains many impurities, but is a raw material for cast iron and wrought iron.

Cast iron is made from pig iron by resmelting it with coke in a blast furnace. The coke raises the temperature and helps remove the impurities. The molten cast iron is tapped from the base of the furnace and poured into moulds. Although it is brittle, cast iron melts and moulds easily. Because it does not distort when red hot and corrodes only slightly in water, cast iron is used for stoves, fireplaces, manhole covers, water pipes and rain gutters.

If cast iron is resmelted, the result is wrought iron—an almost pure form of iron, which is not much made today. It can be easily shaped (or wrought) and, until the 1870s, was used for bridge building and engineering. Nowadays it is used mostly for decorative purposes. It gave way to the master-metal steel, which was first mass produced in the 1870s and which combines the easy-to-handle qualities of wrought iron with the toughness of cast iron.

## BATHROOM ELECTRICS

It is dangerous to take electrical appliances into a bathroom or indeed anywhere that there is a lot of moisture, because water is such an excellent conductor of electricity. A person could receive an extremely severe, if not fatal, electric shock if the appliance fell into the bathwater.

There are two kinds of electricity. One is static electricity which remains stationary in an object. The other is current electricity which flows, as in a wire. An electric current is formed by the movements of electrons. It is possible to transfer electrons from one thing to another by rubbing them together. One object is given a positive charge, and the other a negative charge of electricity. Objects with like charges repel each other while those with unlike charges attract each other.

Some things lose their charge at once. Others retain it for a long time. Substances which do not retain an electrical charge are called conductors, while those which keep the charge are called non-conductors or insulators. All metals and water are conductors. The human body is also a conductor, but not a good one. Insulators include glass, paper, plastic and silk. In fact, materials which are good conductors of heat are also conductors of electricity.

Water is at least a million times better at conducting electricity at room temperature than any other non-metallic liquid. So never take the risk of a terrible accident by handling any electrical gadget in the bath. You should also remember to turn off the current before touching anyone who has had an electric shock and is still in contact with the appliance. If you don't do this you will probably get a shock too!

# WHY is DDT dangerous?  WHY do pipes sometimes burs

# WHY is a screw so strong?  WHY do road vehicles hav

## DDT

After extensive use as a pesticide, DDT was found to have many harmful after-effects on human beings and animals. The control of insects was revolutionized by the introduction of DDT after the Second World War. It was employed to combat a wide range of insects which attacked food crops and was also instrumental in bringing the world malaria problem under control.

But by the 1960s it was found that DDT affected the metabolism of many birds so much that their eggs became too fragile to survive. As a result many species have nearly become extinct. Several kinds of fish have also been seriously affected. Large numbers of insects which served as food for both fish and birds have been destroyed. The effects of DDT on food for human consumption have been extremely serious. Food becomes poisonous if the amount of DDT in it exceeds a certain limit. However, such pesticides are now heavily restricted by most governments.

## BURST PIPES

Cold water pipes may burst in winter when the outside temperature falls below 0° Centigrade (32° Fahrenheit) and the water turns to ice. The pipe's walls crack to relieve the pressure caused by the fact that ice requires nearly one-tenth more space than the water. One cubic foot of water makes 1·09 cubic feet of ice. To prevent a freeze-up, a heat insulator is wrapped round the pipes.

Water has very unusual properties. Apart from expanding when frozen, it requires more heat to warm it than any other common substance. In other words it has a high specific heat. In nature there are some obvious advantages in these peculiarities. The expansion of ice causes the breaking up of clods of water-filled soil on cold winter nights to leave a fine tilth admirably suited to spring sowing. Water's high specific heat means that the sea takes longer to warm up than the land and longer to cool down. Thus the sea acts to prevent extreme changes in temperature between the seasons.

## STRENGTH OF SCREW

The screw provides a means of converting a small force into a large one. Once in use, it allows pressure to be applied from different directions. These factors give the screw its relative strength as compared with a nail of the same size.

In the first case, the force applied to a screw is like the smaller force necessary to lift an object up an inclined plane rather than straight up. In a screw a form of inclined plane is provided by the spiral groove, called a thread, which is cut round the shaft. By contrast the force applied to a nail can be compared with lifting an object straight up. If it were possible to unwind an inch-long screw, you would find that it was longer than an inch-long nail.

In the second case, the holding power of a screw or nail in a piece of wood depends on the pressure exerted on its shank by the wood fibres. A screw creates a far stronger grip because it presents a much greater surface area to the pressure of the wood.

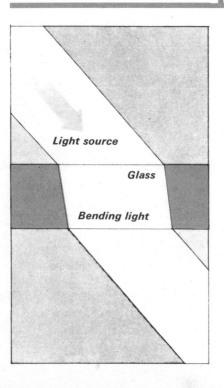

Light source

Glass

Bending light

## GLASS

We can see through glass because it allows the light rays to pass through. Glass is a hard, brittle material made by fusing silica with the oxides or silicates of such metals as sodium, magnesium, calcium and potassium. The product is cooled rapidly to prevent the formation of any crystalline material which would interfere with the passage of light. The melting point of glass is about 800–950° Centigrade (1,472–1,742° Fahrenheit).

In fact, light does not travel straight through glass but is bent or refracted. The light is bent twice, first when it enters the glass and then back to its original direction. when it comes out at the other side. Every transparent material bends light, but the amount (described by a number called the index of refraction) varies with the density of the material. The denser the material, the greater is the amount of bending and the higher the index. The speed of light also varies as it enters another material becoming slower as the density of the material increases.

The ability of glass to refract light rays has made possible the designing of lenses which are essential for the important science of optics. A convex lens—a lens with one or both of its surfaces bulging outward—bends light rays inward. A concave lens—with one or both of its surfaces curving inward—spreads light rays outward.

in winter? **WHY** can we see through glass?
•neumatic tyres? **WHY** does frozen food keep for a long time?

## PNEUMATIC TYRES

Pneumatic tyres help to cushion the vehicle against bumps, ruts and other inequalities in the road surface. This levelling effect of the tyre is achieved because of the compressed air which is inside the rubber casing.

Until about 1900 all road vehicles were fitted with solid tyres. These were very unsatisfactory. When a tyre struck an obstacle on the road surface the shock often damaged the vehicle's mechanism permanently. In any case the effect was most uncomfortable for the passengers, and the roads then had holes and potmarks, which made driving over them dangerous.

The adaptability of pneumatic tyres gives them a firmer grip on the road and enables the driver to steer, change speed and go round corners more safely.

## FROZEN FOOD

Frozen food keeps for a long time because the freezing of the water inside the food forces the bacteria, which cause it to decompose, into inactivity. Like all living things, bacteria need water in order to thrive.

Bacteria are microscopic organisms, or forms of life which occur in air, water and soil all over the world. But they flourish and multiply particularly wherever organic matter is present. Some may cause disease, others are harmless, or even beneficial, but their activity causes organic matter, including food, to decompose.

Modern discoveries have enabled sub-zero temperatures to be obtained by cooling air to about −300° Centigrade (−508° Fahrenheit) by compressing it and passing it into low pressure chambers through fine nozzles. The result is a sudden and violent expansion, causing the air to be drastically cooled. In home refrigerators Freon-12 gas is used instead of air, and the temperatures are much less drastic. The temperature in the freezing compartment of a domestic refrigerator is about −4°C or 25°F, and that of a deep-freezer about −15°C or 5°F.

Preserving food has an ancient history. The salting and smoking of fish and meat have been carried out for centuries. Another long-used method of preserving food is to change its form, for example turning milk into butter and cheese, and grapes into wine. More recently preservation has been effected by canning, heat being used to kill bacteria, or dehydration.

Most fresh food contains 75 to 90 per cent of water. When this liquid is removed, great savings in packaging, storage and transport are made. Potatoes, milk, eggs, tea and coffee are among the well-known products now sold as dry powders that need only the addition of water to reconstitute them.

# WHY does a space capsule need a heat-shield? WHY do
# WHY does smoke go up the chimney?

## SPACE CAPSULE

A space capsule needs a heat-shield to protect it and its occupants from the extremely high temperatures generated by its friction with the earth's atmosphere.

The space capsule starts its return journey to earth at a very high speed. The temperature of the craft's skin rises rapidly as it meets the resistance of the denser air near the earth. The heat turns the colour of the shield red and then bright orange, before the craft is slowed down enough for the final descent to earth.

Without its heat-shield the craft would disintegrate into a long white trail of melting metal—in the same way that meteorites do when they plunge through the atmosphere of the earth.

## FLUORIDE

Drinking water containing fluoride, or, to be more exact, sodium fluoride, is generally believed to help in preventing dental trouble.

It was not until the late 1930s that efforts to combat tooth decay involved the use of chemical substances. The addition of a small amount of fluoride—about one part in a million—to the drinking water of a community, has been linked with a reduction in tooth decay, sometimes as great as 60 per cent.

Sodium fluoride interferes with the chain of reactions which causes acid to be formed on the teeth. Also it helps the teeth become more resistant to these mouth acids. It should be pointed out, however, that too much fluoride in the water is likely to produce mottling and, in severe cases, decay of the tooth enamel.

## G-FORCES

G-forces occur when any object tries to escape from the earth. An object thrown into the air will fall back again because of the earth's gravitational pull.

The force of this pull depends upon the mass, or weight, of the object and its distance from the earth's centre. This attraction would give any object falling freely without air resistance an acceleration of 9·8 metres or 32 feet a second. Thus if it was travelling at 22 m.p.h. at the end of the first second, it would be travelling at 44 m.p.h. at the end of the next second and at 66 m.p.h. at the end of the third second.

The gravitational pull of the earth gives us our apparent weight and is usually referred to as 1G or G. So if we hear that a rocket or space-craft is accelerating at 2G it means that it is making everything on it appear to be twice as heavy as it usually is.

The escape speed, or escape velocity, needed to get away from the pull of the earth's gravity is about 25,000 m.p.h. Even this speed would not put the space-craft entirely beyond all pull of gravity, because our gravitational field reaches out to infinity. But the pull becomes weaker as the distance from earth increases.

1/16g
16,000 miles

1/9g
12,000 miles

$\frac{1}{4}$g

8,000 miles from centre of earth

g
Earth

## CHIMNEY SMOKE

Smoke will rise up the chimney or through the nearest opening it can find because it is hotter and, therefore, lighter than the air in the room.

Before the days of chimneys smoke was allowed to escape through vents or open turrets in the roof. Chimneys were introduced to induce a draught, thus providing more air for the fire. The hot smoke passing up the shaft made room for cool air, of higher density.

Thus a chimney would not only carry away the smoke and gases from a fire but also act as a ventilator enabling a change of air in the room.

## BOILING WATER

Water will boil at varying temperatures depending on the pressure of the atmosphere. But once it has reached its relative boiling point it will not rise in temperature, however much more heat is applied. All the heat is absorbed in turning the water into steam. In the 18th Century, Joseph Black explained this occurrence with his theory that the heat becomes "latent"—or lies hidden—in the steam.

When the pressure on the container is increased above normal atmospheric pressure, the heat required to boil the water will be greater. This is because boiling water consists of innumerable molecules agitated by the heat to such an extent that they move fast enough to break free from the restraining force that holds the water together. As the pressure exerted on the water is increased, the greater must be the agitation of the molecules for them to burst free and the greater must be the heat needed to achieve such agitation.

Where the atmospheric pressure is less than at sea level, the water will boil at under 212° Fahrenheit (100° Centigrade). At a height of 10,000 feet water boils at 194° Fahrenheit. So the higher one goes up a mountain the harder it is to make water hot enough to boil an egg.

# General Knowledge

### LOCH NESS

Loch Ness is the most famous of all the fresh water lochs in Scotland because of reports that it is inhabited by an aquatic monster.

Since the middle of the 19th Century many local inhabitants and visitors claim to have seen the Loch Ness Monster. In recent years much photographic and documentary evidence has been produced from which some experts have detected a resemblance between the monster and aquatic reptiles that lived more than 50,000 years ago.

Nevertheless, in spite of the stories, official opinion still doubts that such a creature actually exists. Frogmen and submarines have searched in vain for the monster. But it has been pointed out that there are caves and subterranean waterways beneath the surface of Loch Ness leading to other lochs, in which the supposed monster could hide.

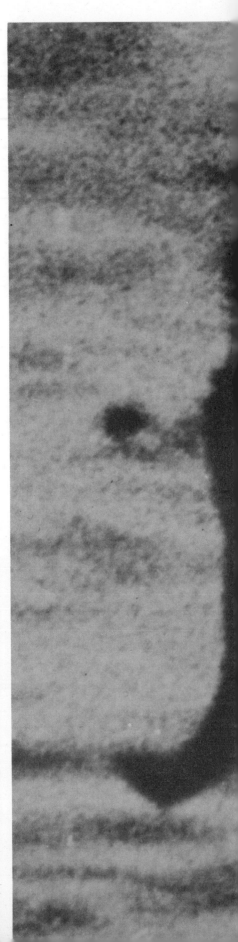

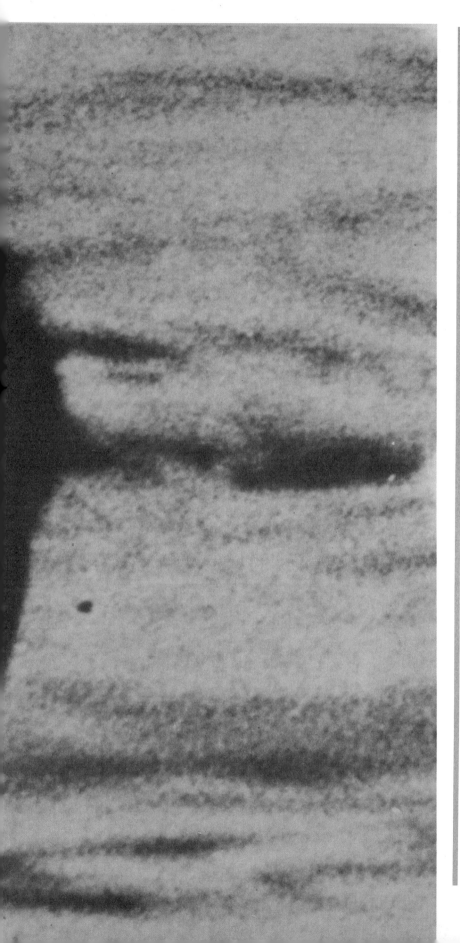

## HERB GARDEN

An important feature of all monasteries in the Middle Ages was the infirmary or home for the sick and the aged, and the herb garden, or herbarium, was there to provide the necessary ingredients for making up medicines.

Herbal medicines, usually derived from the juices of certain plants, have been used since the dawn of history. In the 3rd Century B.C., Theophrastus, a Greek, wrote a "History of Plants". In the 2nd Century A.D., Dioscorides used herbal remedies in his position as official physician to the Roman armies. During the Middle Ages, monks studied the works written by Dioscorides on herbal remedies and added to these the results of their own experiments and practical experience. The oldest established hospitals are direct survivals of the monastic infirmaries of the Middle Ages. The best known exponent of herbal medicines was Nicholas Culpepper (1616–1654), whose book "The Complete Herbal" is still available today.

*Miniature from the 14th-Century* De ruralibus comedia *by Pietro de Crescenzi.*

# WHY do we use double glazing? WHY are Wellington boo... WHY is Confucius so admired?

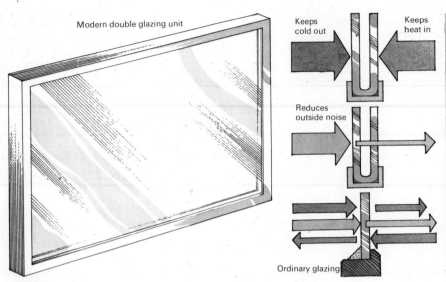

Modern double glazing unit

Keeps cold out    Keeps heat in

Reduces outside noise

Ordinary glazing

*Heat and cold pass through the bottom, unglazed window.*

## DOUBLE GLAZING

Double glazing for windows reduces loss of heat through the glass and cuts down noise from outside. There are many different systems, including some which do not need professional installation, but the principle is the same. Two sheets of glass are fitted together with a constant cushion of air between them.

This glass-air-glass sandwich should, therefore economize on fuel and make the room quieter. It should also reduce condensation, or water on the inside of the window caused by warm air meeting the cold glass. It will make a room more comfortable in winter, especially near the windows, and may even make it more difficult for a burglar to get in.

The efficiency of this insulation (or separation from the cold outside) is effected by the distance between the glass sheets. Heat insulation increases with the air space up to three-quarters of an inch, but a four-inch space is required for effective sound insulation.

Half or even more of the heat that goes out through single windows can be retained by double glazing, but three-quarters of the heat lost from an average house may escape through other outlets.

## WELLINGTON BOOTS

Wellington boots take their name from the first Duke of Wellington. The duke had a special pair designed for him to suit the conditions of his campaigns through Spain and Belgium. No doubt the changes in climate and, in, particular the muddy Belgian fields prompted his desire for tougher footwear.

The original boots reached as far as the knee and were impregnated with waterproofing materials, probably with a rubber base. They were equally suited to walking and to riding.

## SHOE SOLES

The soles of shoes are worn out by the pressure of the feet on the ground. The harder the ground or the rougher the surface, the sooner the soles will wear through.

Every time you walk, tiny particles are scraped off the soles by the ground. To obtain the maximum degree of durability the leather used for soles is compressed. Nowadays this firmness is achieved through the pressure of heavy rolling machines. Before mechanization cobblers hammered layers of leather together.

## CONFUCIUS

Confucius dedicated his life to attempting to relieve the suffering of the people of China, where he lived between 551 and 479 B.C. He was a philosopher and political theorist, whose ideas have deeply influenced the civilization of Eastern Asia.

This great teacher was deeply distressed by the misery he saw on every hand. The Chinese were oppressed by wars, taxes and hunger. Confucius believed the solution must lie in the creation of a form of government which would have as its objective not the pleasure of the rulers, but the happiness of the people.

He advocated such measures as the reduction of taxes, the mitigation of severe punishments and the avoidance of unnecessary war. He tried to secure a position of administrative influence; but in this he failed because the Chinese rulers thought his ideas dangerous. So he taught his beliefs to younger men and sought government posts for these disciples.

Confucius was the first man in China to use teaching as an instrument of reform. But he was not dogmatic or authoritarian. He merely asked questions and insisted that the students found the answers for themselves.

He declared: "If, when I point out one corner of the subject the student cannot work out the other three for himself, I do not go on."

His belief that the state should be a wholly co-operative enterprise was quite different from the ruling ideas of his time. Aristocrats were believed to rule by virtue of the authority and the powerful assistance of their divine ancestors.

The right to govern, Confucius held, depended upon the ability to make the people governed happy.

*Right: A large Shibuichi Tsuba, showing Lao-Tse, Buddha and Confucius.*

# WHY are bodies cremated?  WHY are wedding rings
# WHY do Sikhs wear turbans?  WHY is

## CREMATION

Cremation is the burning of human remains to ashes. Reasons given for adopting this practice include considerations of hygiene, a shortage of land for cemeteries and the rapid growth in population.

Many peoples of the ancient world, including the Greeks and Romans, practised cremation. But in Europe it ceased to be popular with the growth of Christianity and belief in the resurrection of the body.

The modern development of cremation dates from 1874 with the formation of the Cremation Society of England. The society's aim was to replace burial with a method of disposal which would "rapidly resolve the body into its component elements by a process which would not offend the living and would render the remains perfectly innocuous".

The society met with much opposition, and it was not until after the Second World War that local authorities decided to encourage cremation because of the shortage of land. Today cremation is permitted either by law or by custom in about three-quarters of the countries of the world.

## WEDDING RINGS

The modern custom of wearing gold wedding rings originated in Roman times, but the idea took many centuries to become established as a universally accepted tradition. At first rings made of iron were introduced as tokens of betrothal. In those days the privilege of wearing gold rings was reserved for Roman senators and magistrates.

As the Empire became more affluent and permissive, this right was allowed to spread through the various levels of society, and engaged couples took advantage of the freedom to use the coveted gold for their betrothal rings.

A great writer of the early Christian church, Tertullian (about 155–222) said that gold "being the nobler and purer metal and remaining longer uncorrupted was thought to intimate the generous, sincere and durable affection which ought to be between the married parties". Gold marriage rings, as distinct from betrothal rings, came into use from the 5th Century, but do not appear to have been generally adopted by the Church for use in the wedding ceremony until much later. At first they probably simply received the Church's blessing.

In English-speaking countries the wedding ring is usually worn on the third finger of the left hand, perhaps because of an old belief that a nerve ran from that finger directly to the heart. But in Germany and France and other European countries both husband and wife wear the ring on the third finger of the right hand, the hand traditionally used for making vows.

*This large wedding ring is unusually decorated. The smaller engagement ring is worn on the same finger.*

## SIKHS AND TURBANS

Sikhs wear their symbolic turbans because they have long hair. The turban keeps the hair free of dust and dirt and keeps it out of the way so that they can live and work comfortably. The Sikhs' religion, which forbids them to cut their hair, is a mixture of two faiths—the Muslim and Hindu. Drinking and smoking and, indeed, all practises that are bad for the health of the body are banned. The Sikh religion allows both men and women to perform religious ceremonies. The Sikhs believe that all men and women are equal.

At the Hindu New Year in 1699, the Guru (or teacher) Gobind Rai, assembled his followers in the foothills of the Himalayas and initiated five of them as members of a fraternity which he named Khalsa, which means pure. They drank amrit (nectar) out of the same bowl, although they all came from different castes. Also, they received new names with the suffix Singh (lion) and swore to keep the five K's which were: to wear long hair (kesh), a comb (kangha) in the hair, soldiers' shorts (kachha), a steel bangle (kara) on the right wrist, and a sabre (kirpan).

In the days that followed, 80,000 people were initiated into the Khalsa fraternity.

Sikh boys and girls now undergo the initiation ceremony of the five K's at the age of puberty. Boys take the additional name of Singh, but not all persons named Singh are Sikhs. The corresponding name for Sikh women is Kaur.

The Sikhs are excellent farmers, soldiers and mechanics. The proportion of literacy among them is higher than among any of the other major communities of India.

raditionally made of gold?

eonardo da Vinci so famous? **WHY** do we need passports?

## LEONARDO DA VINCI

Leonardo da Vinci is the perfect example of the all-round educated man of the Renaissance. Born in Florence in 1452, he soon became famous for his remarkable paintings. His painting the "Mona Lisa", now in the Louvre, Paris, is possibly the best known painting in the world.

His enormous talents encompassed a wide variety of subjects ranging from sculpture to military engineering. He devoted much time to the concept of flying machines and carried out experiments, without success, in this field. From his work as an artist he developed a knowledge both of anatomy and of the science of light. His anatomical drawings are of a rare beauty and of great precision.

Leonardo was also knowledgeable on such varied subjects as astronomy, geology, botany, and geography. In architecture his studies produced both beautiful designs and practical scientific information. The great man's interests were so diverse that he even gave specific and most serious instructions on how to make and launch stink bombs.

## PASSPORTS

Passports have been used for centuries as a means of identifying and protecting people travelling in foreign countries in times of both peace and war. But the adoption of the passport as an essential travel document is fairly recent.

The development of compulsory passports was accompanied by the introduction of visas. These are endorsements by officials of foreign states that entry is permitted.

Originally a passport, as the word indicates, meant permission to leave a port or to sail into it. Later this was extended to include a general permission of exit and entry.

# WHY does the tower of Pisa lean?   WHY is there a U-ber

## TOWER OF PISA

The tower of Pisa is the bell tower of the cathedral of Pisa in Tuscany, Italy. It leans because, when the building was half completed, the soil under one half of the circular structure began to subside and the tower tipped.

Work on the tower was begun in 1173, but was discontinued for a century after the subsidence. However, in 1275 architects devised a plan to compensate for the tilt. Two storeys, the third and the fifth, were built out of line with the others and closer to the vertical in an effort to alter the tower's centre of gravity.

But the leaning has continued to increase gradually throughout the centuries. Pumping to keep water away from the surrounding ground and the injection of cement grout into the foundations and the surrounding subsoil have been tried in recent years, but without success.

The tower, which is one of the most unusual in existence, is Romanesque in style and made of white marble. It is cylindrical in shape and has eight storeys.

The tilt is about 17 feet, or more than five degrees from the perpendicular. The tower continues to increase its tilt by about a quarter of an inch each year.

## U-BEND

U-bend pipes are installed under sinks and toilets to provide a water seal against the outside sewer pipes. The U-bend retains a permanent pool of clean water, protects the fixture and prevents any gases, vermin or bacteria from escaping out of the sewers.

The U-bend was invented in the middle of the 18th Century but, for economic reasons, was not widely used until more than 100 years later. Since its introduction the U-bend has been an important factor in preventing infectious illnesses and diseases in large cities.

elow a sink or toilet?

WHY is the Ganges considered to be sacred?

## GANGES

The River Ganges is considered sacred by more than 200 million people because of its part in the observance of the oldest organized religion existing in the world, the 3,500-year-old religion of Hinduism. For century after century hundreds of thousands of pilgrims have visited its shores every year to wash away their sins in the muddy waters. Brahmans and outcasts, kings and beggars, people of every caste and race of Hindu India have swarmed down stone steps to wade in "Mother Ganga" for spiritual purification and the good of their souls.

Devout Hindus hope to die on its shores and have their ashes strewn on the surface of the holy river. For those unable to make the pilgrimage quantities of the water are widely distributed and preserved to be drunk as the hour of death approaches.

The most sanctified spot of the sacred Ganges is the ancient city of Benares with its 1,500 temples, countless idols, and a four-mile curve of ghats, or steps, leading down to the river.

Apart from the pilgrims, many boats and steamers gather in the Ganges because it is also a great commercial highway. The vast plain which it crosses in a gentle gradient is a maze of life-giving irrigation projects, for more people live there than in any other river valley except the Yangtze in China.

The source of the Ganges is usually given as the Bhagirathi which gushes from an ice cave more than two miles above sea-level. It flows from west to east for 1,540 miles and drains an area of 430,000 square miles. Finally it pours its silt-laden waters into the Bay of Bengal. Here is the most extensive delta in the world, a fan-shaped formation which the Ganges shares with another river, the Brahmaputra, after the latter's southward sweep from Tibet.

# WHY does a trumpet have valves?　WHY is glue sticky?
# WHY do tennis racquets have strings?

## TRUMPET VALVES

Valves in a trumpet enable the player to lower, momentarily, the pitch of the note he wishes to to make. What happens when one of the valves is pushed down is that the air is diverted through a small loop of tube thus lowering the pitch or sound of the instrument.

When the first valve is pressed, usually by the first finger, the pitch of the trumpet will be lowered by a whole tone. The second valve, according to the same principle, lowers the sound by a semitone, and the third lowers it by a minor third.

Nearly all trumpets and brass instruments today are made with valves. The mechanism was invented in 1815 by two Germans. Today most valves are of the piston type with springs to return the valves to their original position.

The history of trumpets dates back to 1500 B.C. in Egypt. But until the beginning of the 19th Century all the variations produced by valves had to be made by the player controlling his breath.

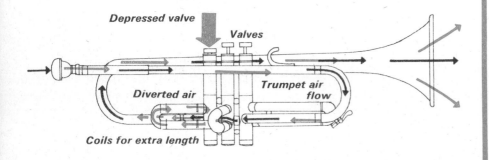

Depressed valve　Valves

Diverted air　Trumpet air flow

Coils for extra length

## GLUE

The chemical and physical processes which cause glue to stick are still not completely understood. So the manufacture of adhesives tends to be based largely on experiment rather than on theory.

Usually it is easier to stick together two porous objects such as paper or wood. The glue will enter the tiny pores of the material, then dry and solidify to form a grip.

For metals, synthetic glues are required. It helps to roughen the surface slightly, since there are no natural openings for the adhesive. Synthetic glues were not developed until the 1930s but natural glues such as rubber or beeswax, have been used since prehistoric times. Discoveries in ancient tombs showed the early Egyptians used animal glues to make furniture and attach ornaments to wood surfaces.

## LASCAUX

The Lascaux caves in south-western France contain some of the finest examples of prehistoric art. These are mural paintings dating back about 15,000 years and representing the very beginning of European culture.

The caves were discovered in 1940 in the Dordogne region. Their impressive frescos depict—in a startlingly modern style—ancient hunting expeditions, bulls, horses, deer and wild fowl. It has been suggested that the art had a definite function—that the animal pictures were believed to ensure the success in hunting necessary for the painters.

The limited amount of air in the caves and the humidity generated by the visitors caused the paintings to begin to deteriorate. So the caves have had to be closed to all except archaeologists, and tourists must be satisfied with expert reproductions in caves nearby, where great care has been taken to simulate the colours of the original paintings.

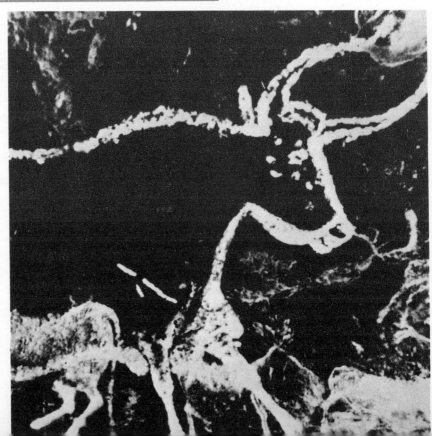

# WHY is Lascaux famous?
## WHY do some coins have a milled edge?

## TENNIS RACQUETS

As long ago as the 11th Century games similar to tennis were being played with racquets. These racquets were already made with strings of plaited catgut to provide a light, strong and springy surface.

Solid racquets, presumably made entirely of wood, were used in ancient Egypt and Persia. But they must have been extremely unwieldy and probably damaged beyond repair after a few games.

Some early racquets were strung diagonally in diamond shapes. The present vertical and horizontal network was adopted because it gave greater resistance.

Several grades of gut are used in modern tennis, varying in thickness, resiliency and adaptability. The tension of the stringing can be adjusted. The lighter the strings the faster the ball leaves the racquet, but the more difficult it is to control. Looser stringing makes it easier to cut the ball.

## COINS

The practice of minting coins with a milled or raised edge dates back to the 15th Century. It was introduced to protect the design on both faces of the coins, by leaving them slightly below the edge. Also, this made it easier to stack them.

Any peculiarity of a coin, such as a raised edge, makes forgery more difficult. Only the complicated machinery in the possession of the national mint can produce coins with accurately milled edges.

## EASTER EGGS

Easter eggs provide one of the many popular traditions that have grown up around the great spring celebration in the Christian calendar of the resurrection of Christ. During the period of Lent preceding Easter eggs were forbidden as part of the fast in preparation for the festival. So it was natural for the end of Lent to be marked by the eating of eggs on Easter Sunday.

As traditional symbols of life and creation eggs suggested the resurrection. The decorations on the eggs can be regarded as symbolizing the end of the penitential season and the beginning of joyful celebration.

Sometimes eggs are blessed in church. Egg-rolling and egg-hunting are two self-descriptive Easter games. An expensive custom developed in Imperial Russia, where the nobility exchanged egg-shaped curios made of precious materials and decorated with jewels. These "eggs" are now extremely valuable.

Many of the folk customs and traditions now associated with Easter may be adaptations of practices connected with pagan spring ceremonies. So eggs coloured like the rays of the sun may have originally symbolized the return of spring.

## GOLF CLUBS

Golfers' clubs can be divided into four basic classes: drivers, irons, spoons and putters. All four are shaped for different purposes and are used according to the ground the golfer is playing on and the shot he intends to make.

Wooden drivers are used for the first stroke from the tee. Spoons are designed chiefly to get a ball out of a rut. Various irons are selected for the approach to the green, where the putter is brought into play for the final shots.

Usually a good player's set will include seven to ten irons and three to four wood clubs. The different clubs are known by both number and name. Wood clubs are numbered one to five—the fifth sometimes replacing an iron—and irons from one to ten. No more than 14 clubs should be carried by a player during a round.

*Details from* above *Compotier aux Poires and* right *Crouching Woman.*

## PICASSO

Pablo Ruiz Picasso was a Spanish painter, sculptor and engraver who lived from 1881 to 1973. He was a very independent artist and, with another painter called George Braque, founded a whole new movement in art which became known as Cubism.

At a very early age he showed exceptional talent. He went to the School of Fine Art in Barcelona and to the Academy of San Fernando in Madrid. Eventually, in 1905, he established himself in Paris.

Between 1899 and 1905 his first subjects were lively scenes of popular and bourgeois life—cabarets, racecourses, dance halls. Later he changed to depicting the victims of society—prostitutes, beggars, drunkards, the blind and the crippled.

He tried to get closer to what he felt was reality by approaching his subjects from several different angles. He extracted new meanings from them and employed the fullest possible range of expressive techniques.

Eventually he started a new way of pictorial representation based on a shifting viewpoint, a free approach to colour and the right to show what one knows instead of what the eye sees. This was the start of Cubism which was an alternative pictorial language to naturalism.

He went through many changes of style and awareness, and his contribution to the world of art has been immense and revolutionary. His paintings are highly valued throughout the world.

different clubs?

**WHY** was Picasso considered to be such a great painter?

# WHY are there so many skyscrapers in New York?

## SKYSCRAPERS

There are so many skyscrapers in New York because these enormous buildings are able to accommodate hundreds of people on their many storeys while taking up only a relatively small amount of land — and New York is short of land.

The skyscrapers are found in the heart of New York City, the centre of its business, financial and entertainment activities, which are all packed into an area of 10 square miles on the lower half of Manhattan Island, between the Hudson and East Rivers. The lack of space makes the value of land tremendously high and therefore the building of tall structures has become a necessity.

Manhattan is shaped rather like a tongue and is made of solid

granite. The skyscrapers are grouped in two great clusters, the lower group standing at the southern tip of the island, looking down across Upper New York Bay towards the Atlantic and making up the famous New York skyline which greets visitors by ship to America. This group includes the Woolworth building (792 feet) and the Bank of Manhattan (900 feet).

The upper cluster of buildings is about halfway up the island, in what is known as the 'midtown' section. Here the enormous Empire State building rises to a height of 102 storeys (1,472 feet) and often has its peak wreathed in cloud. Nearby is the Chrysler building (1,046 feet).

# WHY was one group of painters called the Impressionists?

*Detail from Monet's painting of Rouen Cathedral.*

# WHY do fashions in clothes change?

## IMPRESSIONISTS

The term Impressionist is used to describe a new and revolutionary movement in painting which was developed in Paris in the 1870s. The word was first used derisively by critics of the movement, and was taken from Claude Monet's canvas representing the sun rising over the sea and entitled *Impression*. Monet was a central figure in the development of the Impressionist movement, along with Manet, Degas, Renoir, Pissarro, Sisley, Cezanne, Guillaumin and Berthe Morisot.

What these painters tried to do was to get away from the romanticism and the fetters of the accepted artistic convention. Experiments were made with the use of the pure colours of the prism and the splitting up of "tone" into its component colours.

The Impressionists painted outdoor modern life and chose as their subjects Paris and urban scenes, the coasts of the English Channel and the North Sea, and the little village resorts along the banks of the Seine and Oise which had been made accessible by railway. They aimed to convey the changing rhythm of light.

## FASHIONS

Fashions in clothes change for almost as many different reasons as there are fashions. Among the chief causes are changes in the kind of work we do, the cost and availability of the materials used and the invention of new materials, such as man-made fibres.

The attitude of different societies towards the body and how much of it should be displayed is also important. For example, if a girl in the Middle Ages had worn a mini-skirt she would have been regarded as either mad or wicked. Social standards change from age to age and from country to country.

There have been dramatic changes in fashion in our century, partly owing to the availability of new and cheap materials and partly because this generation believes that clothes should be a matter of personal choice, and comfortable as well as attractive.

Many of the fussy clothes of our ancestors, often requiring yards and yards of material, would be too expensive to produce today. They would also be unsuited to modern living—imagine cycling in a crinoline!

Great wars often influence fashions. During the Second World War the style of women's clothes became military. Jackets for instance, had square and padded shoulders. After the war, this fashion changed to the voluminous, more feminine, new look of Dior, the great French designer.

Another big change happened after the First World War. Women who had worked for the first time with men in the factories during the war, began to dress with greater freedom and started to wear short skirts.

Today, what we wear is largely a matter of personal choice, convenience and what we can afford.

# WHY do we have police? WHY is holly used at Christmas

## POLICE

Every society, with very few exceptions, has some form of police force. The chief function of the police is to protect society and the individual from the criminal and the criminally insane. Their duty is to ensure the maintenance of public order and the protection of the citizen and his property.

Unfortunately many police forces have existed, throughout history, which have exceeded their basic duties of protection and have persecuted people and organizations on political or racial grounds. A notable example was the Gestapo of Hitler's Germany.

The first recognizably modern police force was established in Britain in 1829 by Sir Robert Peel, whose policemen were given the nickname of Peelers or Bobbies.

# WHY do people kiss under the mistletoe?
# WHY are monks tonsured?

## CHRISTMAS HOLLY

The custom of having holly in the house at Christmas probably comes from the old Germanic races of Europe who used to hang evergreen plants indoors during the winter as a refuge for the spirits of the forest.

Also, holly was considered to be a symbol of survival by the pre-Christian Romans and was much used as a decoration during their Saturnalia festival which was held at the end of December.

The Germanic Yuletide celebrations took place at the same time of the year. So when people began to celebrate Christmas the feast of the Nativity of Christ, many of the older customs were preserved.

Popular superstitions about holly still survive. Some people consider it extremely unlucky to bring holly into the house before Christmas Eve. Another idea depended on the belief that prickly and non-prickly kinds of holly were respectively male and female. So the kind of holly used for decoration decided whether husband or wife would be master of the household over Christmas.

## MISTLETOE

From the earliest times mistletoe was regarded as a bestower of life and fertility. The common mistletoe is one of the most "magical" plants of European folklore.

The mistletoe of the sacred oak was especially venerated by the ancient Celtic Druids. The Druid rite of plucking the mistletoe, described by Julius Caesar, adds an aura of mystery to the magical folklore surrounding the plant.

Decorating the house with mistletoe may be a survival of the old Druid oak cult. The custom is also associated with certain primitive marriage rites.

## MONKS' TONSURE

Tonsure is the name given to the rite of shaving the crown of the head of a cleric entering certain religious orders. It is particularly associated with monks and is a sign of dedication to religious observance.

In the Eastern Orthodox Church tonsure was practised as early as the 4th Century. Prayers of the 9th Century which accompanied such ceremonies show clearly that tonsure was regarded as an outward manifestation of the casting off of earthly values and vanities to dedicate oneself to the service of God.

There are three kinds of tonsure: the Roman type consists in shaving the whole head, leaving only a fringe of hair supposed to symbolize the crown of thorns. The Eastern or Greek style used to involve shaving the entire head, but is now held to have been observed if the hair is closely shorn. The Celtic tonsure means shaving in front of a line stretching over the top of the head from ear to ear.

Long before Christianity there was a religious practice among the Romans and Semites of cutting some of the hair and offering it to a deity as a sign of dedication.

# WHY was the Statue of Liberty built? WHY are horses

# measured in hands?

## STATUE OF LIBERTY

The Statue of Liberty was built to celebrate the birth of the United States of America and to commemorate the friendship between that republic and the republic of France.

It stands on Bedloe's Island (now renamed Liberty Island) at the mouth of New York harbour, in accordance with the wishes of the sculptor Frederic Bartholdi.

The plan for the monument originated in France. The cost of the statue was met by the French people, while the money for the 300-foot pedestal was raised in the United States.

Although the monument was not unveiled until 1886, the idea was conceived at the end of the 18th Century when France and the United States were the only big democratic republics in existence.

Under the 150-foot statue, symbol of freedom and equality, is a moving poem, inscribed inside the pedestal. In this poem *The New Colossus*, the writer, Emma Lazarus, invited the tired, poor and homeless to come to America in search of liberty.

## HORSES

Before man invented rulers and tape measures he often used his hands and feet to express the size of things. An old book published in 1561 says: "Foure graines of barlye make a fynger; foure fyngers a hande; foure hands a foote".

Today horses are still measured in hands. The measurement is taken from the ground to the withers, which is the highest part of the back lying between the shoulder blades.

A hand is reckoned to be four inches, the assumed width of a man's palm. Formerly it was taken as equal to three inches, when a man's hand was smaller.

Early horses were probably around 12 hands (48 inches) at the withers, and one measuring 14 hands was exceptional. Some modern horses, however, reach 17 hands and occasionally 20 hands. A small horse under 14·2 hands is called a pony.

## SHINTO PRIESTS

Shinto is a complex of ancient Japanese folk beliefs and rituals which form the basis of the religion of Japan. Priesthood is hereditary, and priests of major shrines may be from noble families. The priests perform rites of purification and fertility, and formally present newly married couples and infants to the Kami.

The Kami is the unifying concept of God. It is a kind of spiritual power, general and impersonal. It includes the many deities of the heavens and the earth, spirits, birds, beasts, trees, seas and mountains—even evil and mysterious things if they are extraordinary and dreadful.

Also in the Kami are sacred emperors, persons in authority, thunder, foxes, wolves and peaches (sex symbols). So are ancestral spirits, brave warriors and "magical" objects such as mirrors, paper and hair.

In the 6th Century, Buddhism was imported from Korea and gained a great deal of prestige. The two religions were combined to make one form of worship called Ryobu Shinto (two-aspect Shinto). Buddhist and Shinto shrines were merged and the priests performed rites in both religions. However, in the 17th Century scholars rediscovered ancient documents and laid the foundations of modern Shinto.

## OLYMPIC FLAG

The flag used at the Olympic Games has a white background with five interlaced circles representing the five inhabited continents: Africa, America, Asia, Australasia and Europe. Each symbol has a different colour: red, yellow, green, black and blue. But the colours are merely decorative and in no way represent particular continents.

## HOLLYWOOD

Hollywood is the centre of the United States motion picture and television industries. Its situation in the north-west of Los Angeles, California, provided many attractions for pioneers of the film industry at the beginning of this century. The climate was ideal with maximum sunshine and mild tempera-ture. The terrain was well suited with ocean, mountains and desert. And a large labour market was available.

One of Hollywood's first movies to tell a story was *The Count of Monte Cristo*, begun in 1908. By the end of 1911 there were more than 15 producing companies in

the area. Among the famous people working in Hollywood at the beginning of the First World War were Charlie Chaplin, Samuel Goldwyn, Douglas Fairbanks and Cecil B. de Mille.

The advent of the talkie forced many famous stars of the silent screen to retire. But the greatest threat to Hollywood came from television after the Second World War. Many production companies disappeared. Others survived and learned to meet the competition by also making television films.

Today Hollywood is not only the centre of the motion picture industry, but also of the television, film and recording industries of America.

The illustration above shows a magnificent scene from D. W. Griffiths epic film *Intolerance*, made in about 1916 and generally accepted by film buffs, and the public, as one of the great classic films of all time.

# ACKNOWLEDGEMENTS

The publishers would like to thank the following organizations and individuals for their kind permission to reproduce the pictures in this book:

**Associated Newspapers**   106/7 bottom left

**Associated Press**   50

**Australian News & Information Bureau**   31

**Barnaby's Picture Library**   14 bottom (J. E. Downard), 15 (H. C. Harridge), 20 top (W. Thompson), 23, 27 top centre, 44/45, 51, 54/55 top, 54 centre, 55, 57, 72 centre left, 73 top left, 73 centre left and Cover, 79 (Cyril Bernard), 81, 89 right, 91, 96, 97, 101, 106 bottom, 110, 112 (Ann Nowlem), 114 (Sir George Pollock), 123

**Camera Press**   39, 43

**Michael Chinery**   8

**Cinema Bookshop**   126/127

**Bruce Coleman**   12 (John Markham), 16 (Peter Jackson), 17

**Colorific**   13 left (Alan Clifton)

**Daily Telegraph Colour Library**   60

**Mary Evans Picture Library**   35, 42, 47

**Robert Harding**   36

**Michael Holford**   53, 84/85, 109 and Cover, 121

**Eric Hosking**   14 top

**Institute of Ophthalmology**   76

**Keystone**   66/67, 75 left. 75 right, 115, 118/119, 122 right, 122 left

**Frank Lane**   21 (Heinz Schremp), 22 top (Wilford L. Miller), 22 bottom, 24 bottom, 25, 26 left, 26 right, 28, 93 (P. Kirkpatrick)

**William MacQuitty**   52

**Mansell Collection**   34, 62, 78, 111

**NASA**   104

**NHPA**   29 (Douglas Dickins)

**Orbis Publishing**/Library of Congress   33

**Phillips Art Dealers Auctioneers**   49 and Cover

**Picturepoint**   1, 72 left, 72 right, 100 bottom, 124

**Popperfoto**   46, 70, 90, 98

**Pye of Cambridge**   99

**Spectrum Colour Library**   11 (H. C. Harridge), 13 right top, 18 left, 19, 20 bottom, 24 top, 27 bottom, 30, 40/41, 64 top, 64 bottom, 65 top, 65 bottom, 77, 88, 89 left, 95, 100 top, 113, 117, 125

**Joseph Ziolo**   116 (G. Nimatallahy), 120 (André Held)

**Illustrations by Ben and Stephanie Manchipp**